ABUNDANCE

The Poiema Poetry Series

Poems are windows into worlds; windows into beauty, goodness, and truth; windows into understandings that won't twist themselves into tidy dogmatic statements; windows into experiences. We can do more than merely peer into such windows; with a little effort we can fling open the casements, and leap over the sills into the heart of these worlds. We are also led into familiar places of hurt, confusion, and disappointment, but we arrive in the poet's company. Poetry is a partnership between poet and reader, seeking together to gain something of value—to get at something important.

Ephesians 2:10 says, "We are God's workmanship..." *poiema* in Greek—the thing that has been made, the masterpiece, the poem. The Poiema Poetry Series presents the work of gifted poets who take Christian faith seriously, and demonstrate in whose image we have been made through their creativity and craftsmanship.

These poets are recent participants in the ancient tradition of David, Asaph, Isaiah, and John the Revelator. The thread can be followed through the centuries—through the diverse poetic visions of Dante, Bernard of Clairvaux, Donne, Herbert, Milton, Hopkins, Eliot, R. S. Thomas, and Denise Levertov—down to the poet whose work is in your hand. With the selection of this volume you are entering this enduring tradition, and as a reader contributing to it.

—D.S. Martin
Series Editor

Abundance

NEW & SELECTED POEMS

ANDREW LANSDOWN

CASCADE *Books* • Eugene, Oregon

ABUNDANCE
New and Selected Poems

Poiema Poetry Series

Copyright © Andrew Lansdown 2020. All rights reserved. Except for brief quotations in critical publications or reviews, no part of this book may be reproduced in any manner without prior written permission from the publisher. Write: Permissions, Wipf and Stock Publishers, 199 W. 8th Ave., Suite 3, Eugene, OR 97401.

Cascade Books
An Imprint of Wipf and Stock Publishers
199 W. 8th Ave., Suite 3
Eugene, OR 97401

www.wipfandstock.com

PAPERBACK ISBN: 978-1-7252-8457-9
HARDCOVER ISBN: 978-1-7252-8458-6
EBOOK ISBN: 978-1-7252-8459-3

Cataloguing-in-Publication data:

Names: Lansdown, Andrew.

Title: Abundance : new and selected poems / Andrew Lansdown.

Description: Eugene, OR: Cascade Books, 2020 | Series: Poiema Poetry Series | Includes bibliographical references and index.

Identifiers: ISBN 978-1-7252-8457-9 (paperback) | ISBN 978-1-7252-8458-6 (hardcover) | ISBN 978-1-7252-8459-3 (ebook)

Subjects: LCSH: American poetry.

Classification: PS3603.O8887 S65 2020 (print) | PS3603.O8887 (ebook)

Manufactured in the U.S.A.   NOVEMBER 2, 2020

Other books by Andrew Lansdown

Poetry
Homecoming
Counterpoise
Windfalls
Waking and Always
The Grasshopper Heart
Between Glances
Abiding Things: poems, stories, essays
Fontanelle
Birds in Mind: Australian nature poems
Far from Home: Poems of faith, grief and gladness
The Colour of Life (in *Two Poets*)
Gestures of Love: The fatherhood poems
Inadvertent Things: Poems in traditional Japanese forms
Distillations of Different Lands

Poetry for Children
A Ball of Gold: Poems for children
Allsorts: Poetry tricks and treats

Poetry & Photography
Kyoto Sakura Tanka
Kyoto Momiji Tanka: Poems and photographs of Japan in autumn

Short Stories
The Bowgada Birds
The Dispossessed

Novels
With My Knife
Beyond the Open Door (USA edition of *With My Knife*)
Dragonfox
The Red Dragon
The Chronicles of Klarin

For my American friends

Dwight & Sheila Randall
Jeannette Crain
Tom & Claire Muller
Les & Gretchen Golden

"we went through fire and through water;
yet you have brought us out to a place of abundance"
—PSALM 66:12 (ESV)

"out of the abundance of the heart the mouth speaks"
—MATTHEW 12:34 (ESV)

Contents

from *Counterpoise*
Counterpoise 2
On Poetry 3
Sehnsucht 4
For Philip 5
Black Holes 6
Gone 7
Shell 8
Mercy 9
Death 10
Cricket 10
Terror 11
I Whistle and They Come 12
Crabbing 14
Prawning 15
Behind the Veil 16

from *Windfalls*
A Remembrance of Robins 18
Hawk 19
For the Force of Flame 20
The Woman Who Found the Well 21
Like Stephen 22
Apart from Blood 23
Grief 24

from *Waking and Always*

The Horseshoe Shooter 26
The *Shodō* Egret 27
Sacred Kingfisher 29
Water Tank 30
Poem about Freedom 31
Distortions 32
Dugite 32
Kangaroos Crossing 33
Far from Home, the Blower 34
Sometimes in the Dark 37
In Prison 38
For Fear of Freedom 39
Waiting, Singing 40
Spring Morning with Baby and Birds 41
Lighting a Match 42
In Transit 43
For Grace 45
Ford 46
On Haiku 46
Ford and Trees 47
Snake with Angel 48
Not in Truce 49
Waking and Always 50

from *The Grasshopper Heart*

Into Darkness 52
For the Blind 53
Human Rights Poem for Christmas 54
Golgotha 55
White Gum 56
Bread 57
Marri with Nuts 58
Communion 59
Leaf and Load 60
The Grasshopper Heart 61
Spring, Alfred Cove 62

from *Between Glances*
The Visitor 64
Between Glances 65
Birthday 66
Wine Country 67
Sunshower 68
Sonnet of Thanksgiving 69
Rhyme 70
Mirth with Meaning 71
Grace 72
This Abundance 74
Kangaroos 75
Happiness 77
Courtyard 78
Tea with Susan 78
Reaction to a Retard 79

from *Fontanelle*
The Sleep of the Upright 82
Impression 83
Apples 84
Conception 85
Opulence 86
Fontanelle 87
The Weight of the Baby 88
Homecoming 90
A Thing or Two about Monkeys 91
Mowing 92
Shock 93
Home 94
White Ibis 96
Rose 97
He Knows a Place 98
Pathos 99
Listening to Louis 99
Journey 100
Christmas Tree 101

Parable 103
Painting in the Painting 104
Woman Weeping, Sydney 105
Should the Marauders Come 106
Gladdened by Ibises 107
Boat 109

from *Birds in Mind*
Brimming 112
Birds Bathing 113
Each Lily 113
Sighting 114
Menace 115
Black Cockatoos 116
Irises 117
Croaking 117
Fitting 118
Birds in Mind 119

from *Far from Home*
Healing 122
Hurt 124
Fathers 124
You Gladly 125
The Worship Tanka 126
Path 127
Use 127
Bravery 128
Dignity 128
The God of the Glimpses 129
    By My Word 129
    Two Things Unclean 130
    Behind the Glimpses 131
    Going to Zarephath 132
    Gathering Sticks 133
    At the Sight of Her 134
    One Meal More 136

CONTENTS

from *The Colour of Life*
The Colour of Life 138
Delay 139
The Gravity of the Slight 139
Finishing Up 140
Prayer Against Pain 141
Bird and Bull 142
Signal 142
Human 143
Me 143
Haijin and Violet 144
Heat 146
Worship 147
After Death 148
Prayer 149
End of Day 150

from *Inadvertent Things*
Envy 154
Going Down 154
Meditations on Pain 155
Azure 156
Tweezers 156
Waterlily Haiku 157
Daffodils 158
Binoculars 159
Radiance 159
Beloved 160
Kangaroo Haiku 161
Wren Haiku 162
Stargazing 163
Navigation 163
Squid Haiku 164
Black Dog, Snarling 165
Black Dog, Dozing 165
Creators 166
Seeing the Sound 167

CONTENTS

Purity 167
Small Matters 168
Pause 169
Sheep 169
Samurai 170
Black Bamboo 171
Reflection 172
Seize the Day 172

from *Distillations of Different Lands*
Forgetting 174
Recollections of Dread and Deliverance 175
Afterphase 176
Dove Tanka Triptych 177
Wire Wrens 178
Prank Call 179
Dearly Departed 180
Koi Pond Tanka 181
Reading at Lunchtime 182
T'ao Ch'ien and the End of Things 183
Travelling North 185
Canada Geese Near Canada 186
The Martyred Mother 187
The Crimson Maples 188

New & Uncollected Poems
Visiting Bashō's Grave 190
Didgeridoo Player 191
Incidentals 192
Dip 193
Bamboo Forest, Arashiyama 194
On the Substitution Monkey Charms of Kyoto and Nara 195
Temple Ladle 196
The Bodhisattva's Bib 197
The Mother, the Bosatsu, and the Water Child 198
Jizō Stones by the Three-Storied Pagoda 200
Idol Stones 201
First Blood 201

CONTENTS

Apprehension 202
Windbells at Fushimi Inari Shrine 203
Autumn Maples, Kyoto 205
The Easter Trees 206
Gleam 207
Bamboo Dragonflies 208
Little Endings 209
Bamboo Triptych 210
In the Gardens of the Imperial Palace 211
Faces 212
This Woman 212
This Tinnitus 213
Radiance ['Writing the night away'] 214

Endnotes 215
Acknowledgements 221

from
Counterpoise
1980

Counterpoise

Light refracting on the reach of the river;
gulls and sails embracing the slight wind;
jellyfish clasping the calm water
or bunting the sand in the basking shallows;
posts of wood barnacled and rotten;
small waves lisping upon the shore:
here is an abundance I had forgotten.

And here and there, a scatter of children
scamper across the lawn like leaves
driven before the tempest of their happiness.
Parents and grandparents are at ease
in the shade of trees and in each other's company.
For these people, things I thought we had lost
have never been open to doubt.

As the sun departs, parties arrive for prawning:
light their lanterns and lay out their nets.
The world again seems young and lovely,
values certain and strong: young men
and old men, friends, fathers and sons
in pairs dissolve into the dark water
and toil together in the hope of harvest.

How ignorant I have been
through these last years of learning,
how weighted down on one side of the scale.
The large, deep things are all
in their own ways dark and hard.
Small things are a counterpoise
to lighten and soften the heart.

On Poetry
for William Hart-Smith

As we sit talking
about poetry

my son (still months
from walking)

lounges without a care
on my knee, fronts

my old friend with
a vacant stare,

spasmodically stops
our talking with

a short sigh,
and lifts and drops

his foot rhythmically
on the flat of my thigh.

Sehnsucht

Everyone else is asleep
and I am up this early
only to keep my small son from crying.

I carry him down to the river.
A slight mist lingers by the bend.
Trees stand on their heads in the still water.

Has he seen a river before?
I can't remember.
He raises his hand,

reaching for it.
He looks back at me
to make sure I have seen it.

How can anyone find anything so amazing?
Yet it's not just the river:
stones, leaves, chickens, fire—

things I still love
though they've fallen familiar—
fill him continually with joy and wonder.

'Oo! Oo!' he says
as if it hurts him
here in my arms, seeing the river

for the first time.
And a familiar strangeness
grips my heart

and I sing to him,
'Jesus loves the little children',
to keep from weeping.

For Philip

This is what death has done:
Changed him beyond belief
Made him blind and dumb

Turned him cold to the sun
Blown him away like a leaf:
This is what death has done.

> Can a tune beat time
> On the drum of his ear
> Now silence is the sound
> That alone draws near?

Seeing his form, we are numb:
For whom did we make this wreath?
He is blind and dumb.

We huddle together as one,
Yet each alone in our grief.
This is what death has done.

> Can a maiden dance
> In the chamber of his heart
> Now his blood is still
> And he's set apart?

My mother mourns her son,
But tears are cold relief:
He is blind and dumb.

The words that twist my tongue
Are bitter beyond all grief:
Look what death has done—
Made him blind and dumb!

Will the Day Star rise
To the circle of his sight?
Will his tongue peal praise
To the Father of Light?

Black Holes

Everywhere, death. In deep space
there are giant stars collapsed
into themselves, compressed
by their own weight.
As with a terrible grief,
their gravity is so great
not even light can escape.

It is hard to conceive:
black holes—voids
in the vacuum of space.

How long has it been
since the light left your face?
The heavens, my heart—
still I can't tell them apart.

Gone

'Gone!' our son puzzles,
looking for milk in the cup he's emptied.

'Gone!' he says in amazement,
pointing to the lightbulb I switched off.

'Gone!' he urges, tugging at me
as music stops spinning from the record.

We usually laugh: One word
for so many things! 'Yes,' we say. 'Gone.'

But today it is a burden to us
to be reminded all day long.

We are sealed off from joy,
seared by the news of your death.

Shell

Life is no jewel
to the sea

How unconsciously
it must have cast this shell
this white spiral-shell
onto the beach years ago

Its owner died quickly
leaving the house quite empty
except for a ghost
of a smell, which lingered
about the empty stair-well

Without haste
the wind set to work:

Whispered, snickered,
incited the sand
to a sullen fury—
till every grain
on the beach
had raised its grit
to grind the fragile walls

It lies now a house in ruins:

Nothing left but a newel
jagged with the stumps
of several steps

Mercy

Across the footpath (tidy
as Euclid's brain
bar the rude little daisy
bold between two slabs)
the hose
follows itself   and

coming suddenly upon its end
throws a tantrum
before a regiment of roses.
                              But

back along its torso,
in the middle of the path,
a pin-prick spray
sets the daisy dancing.

Death

Quiet, little bird,
you are not alone. Rest, lie
lightly in my hand.
Take all the solace you can:
death is just a breath away.

Cricket

An amber cricket
makes her way mechanically
across the concrete.
Eggs must be laid and there is
so much dying to be done.

Terror

Terror is multiform.

For the young chickens,
a new noise nearby
or a hawk in the clear sky
crushes them flat to the earth.

For each creature, terror
wears a different uniform.
For man, there are more
than the armies of the world.

For my small son, the neighbour's dog
is terror bounding towards him.
And before I can reach him, he falls,
falls to the ground
in the sheer exultation
of fear. Hugging the hard earth
he screams for burial
as if in the tribulation.

I Whistle and They Come

The boy stands in the middle
of the painting, a tin whistle
in his mouth, a bucket of wheat
in his hand, and bantam hens
flocking to his feet,
stretching out their necks as they run.
And the painting's title extends
its loveliness: 'I Whistle and They Come.'

Why was it included in the selection?
There is no other like this one
among the drawings in the collection
of *Pictures by Chinese Children*.
It alone does not trumpet or tell
the Foreword's claim that the children
'learn socialist cultural subjects well'.

'Let's All Criticise Lin Piao and Confucius'
suggests one drawing, with conscientious
children brandishing their small fists.
'The Army and the People Are One Family' insists
another. And a girl aged seven has drawn
a picture called 'Sparkling Red Stars'
of little children, all in uniform,
wearing army caps, and carrying spears.

'I Whistle and They Come'
is the only one, the only one
among all the paintings
that celebrates God's creation
without the slightest taint
of utility and indoctrination—
that says 'I', and does not assume

as absolute the 'we' of the commune.
This is a small triumph, then,
in the face of the darkest works of men.

And surely these other drawings
boast of dark things indeed.
They celebrate the ignoring
of every simple and lovely human need.
In each one, the seed
of self and personality,
of celebration and spontaneity,
has fallen on the sterile ground
of what some men perceive
and enforce as collective good.
How these children must grieve
over joys they have never understood!

And are the teachers proud
of what they have done?
Does their Party boast aloud:
We Whistle and They Come?

Crabbing

Lights float above the blackness
and sometimes a voice drifts in.

We, too, wade into the water
made cold by the warm night.

Mud sucks at our shoes,
swirls up like ink about our legs.

My friend in his soft-rubber thongs
we comfort with the thought of cobbler.

His wife carries the tilly-lamp.
We huddle in the sanctuary of light,

fearful of what might lurk just out of sight.
Like moths, small fish bunt

blindly against my bare legs.
But the estuary is empty of crabs.

In vain we wander through this wet wilderness
in search of blue manna.

We wallow through the water, joke and
jump when imagination claws our ankles.

Once we saw a large crab
(like a straight-edge or a white bone)

with its arms outstretched
to embrace any threat

flicker ghost-like from our circle of light
into the infinite dark.

Prawning

Entering the black water
we are surprised by light.
The thread of our net
billows into a luminous lace
and our bodies take a faint hue,
become ghostly in incandescent blue.

A million small creatures celebrate
our every movement.
They burst upon our sight
at the slightest beckoning
and scintillate
for a moment in our wake.

The path we have trawled
is gone without a trace,
but before us the river
is latent with light and grace.

Behind the Veil

How often my grandparents allude to death, now.
The simplest plans and preparations for the New Year
they preface and conclude: *If we're still here.*
Age, bodily decrepitude, will not allow
illusion. Before death, all things somehow
become transient and grave. Joy and regret
marry each other at the altar of memory. Who can forget
our mortality? Even youths and social visionaries will bow.

For all this, my grandparents are at peace, hoping for the face
of Christ our Saviour. Death will degrade:
even for the redeemed, this peppercorn must be paid.
But he is the resurrection: they are sure of his power and grace.
Still, they are lonely in the shadow of death.
Oh for his face, hidden by the veil of each breath!

from
Windfalls
1984

A Remembrance of Robins

From the twig where they rested
I saw them flit away: two robins
white-capped and scarlet-breasted.

And for a moment they invested
the countryside with colour
from the twig where they rested.

No flower, no other bird contested
the bright display of these two—both
white-capped and scarlet-breasted.

Without warrant they arrested
me: plum blossoms seemed to bloom
from the twig where they rested.

And in departure they divested
the bush of brightness: bobbing away, robins
white-capped and scarlet-breasted.

Hawk

Hunched in an overcoat of feathers
a hawk on the high wire,
like a snapshot of a shrug.

As easily as he wields the wind in his wings
and clamps small creatures in his claws,
he sheds the world from his shoulders.

For the Force of Flame

For the force of flame, a thousand voices shout:
in the moment of change, each leaf cries out,
leaps up redly, brightly eclipsing the white
stars, before flickering and fading into night.

The moon is a water-smoothed stone on a riverbed,
shimmering beneath the streaming smoke. The crack and cough
of coals counterpoint the flames' stutter. Strangely enough
I remember the voice of the fire, but not the things we said.

We re-affirmed what we already knew: we do not agree on this,
on that. How foolishly we darkened simple pleasures—
friendship, fire, roast potatoes and fish—
with our convoluted talk. Life has its proportions and measures:

I would learn them before my soul cries out to its Creator,
leaps, stuttering with joy and shame, up to my Saviour.

The Woman Who Found the Well
John 4:1–39

Why, it was as if he lowered
a pail into the well of my soul
and brought it back brimming with secrets.
I told him things he already knew
because he first asked
of me a drink—I a Samaritan
and he a Jew.

Then *he* offered *me* a drink
said I should thirst
no more. I said
You have nothing
to draw with and
the well is deep.
But he repeated: Water
within you, welling up.

For a moment I mistook his meaning,
thought I'd not have to come
to this well again
in the dust and heat
after the other women had come and gone.

Like Stephen

Stephen, my son, you are
four before my heart is ready.
How quickly you quit yourself!

Well then, if you must
lose your winsome ways
may you win wisdom, and like

Spirit-filled stone-felled Stephen
may you be very valiant
in our Saviour's service.

Apart from Blood
for my father

I do not know when I first knew
I loved you, but from my youth
I have loved you more and more.

And while, apart from blood,
There are reasons,
Surely one is to the fore:

Your life has spoken
The mysterious grammar of godliness,
The deep logic of love and law.

Father, if in eternity I have a place,
It is because (no matter how jaded)
I first saw Jesus in your face.

Grief

It is nothing tangible, no action, no word that has been said,
Just a feeling that sweeps the soul quite without warning
As a wind brushes the growing grain briefly on a calm morning.
It is a grief, a sudden remembrance that he is dead.

It is a feeling and a fact that God alone may understand.
Though I strain to remember, I long to forget.
But neither gives refuge or relief: either holds sorrow and regret.
He is gone: the cup is broken, the water spilt upon the sand.

Like a haunted theatre, there are lights and sounds in my head.
My mind flicks through old film, jams on an almost forgotten frame:
I see his face, hear his voice—and mine, whispering his name.
And for a moment there is nothing, no one I would rather instead.

It dies quickly, lies lightly like an autumn leaf.
But who knows what winds may flick it up again, this grief?

from
Waking and Always
1987

The Horseshoe Shooter

It is almost dark. A car passes
without its lights on. My son shoots it
with the hook end of his hockey stick.
'It shoots horseshoes,' he says.
I imagine a horseshoe
lobbing neatly onto the peg of the driver's neck.
'Piaow! Piaow!' cries my daughter,
improvising with her finger.
'Was this yours?' The old stick
is a new gift from his grandparents.
'No,' I say. 'It was my brother's.'
'Uncle David's?' My daughter is merely
revising the relationships: Dad's brother, my uncle.
'No. My brother Stephen. He's dead.'
They are both suddenly quiet. Their father
has a brother who is dead. Our father.
'Did you have any other brothers?'
'Yes. Philip.' 'Is he dead?' 'Yes.'
The horseshoe shooter has become a music stick
piping death from the basket of my life.
It rises up, the old snake, flicks
its forked tongue, flares its hood, sways, holds
them mesmerised. 'Were you grown up?'
They are thinking of each other now,
these little children, my son and daughter,
brother and sister. If Dad was a boy when ...
are *we* safe? 'Yes,' I say.
Well, almost. 'Yes, I was grown up.'
They are relieved. But my daughter asks,
'And are you the oldest?'
'Well, I am now.' 'Good,' she says,
as if all uncertainties were now
settled, as if night were now the only darkness
coming upon the world. 'Good.'

The *Shodō* Egret

Engrossed, the egret
on the shore neglects
the glint of whitebait
in the sheet water

at its feet. It does not
note its reflection
needled like a tattoo
on the river's skin,

nor reflect that it
can lie as lightly
on air as an image
on liquid. Today,

fish are no food, light
no enlightenment,
flight no fancy. It seeks
another excellence.

In *shodō*, the Way
of Writing, the egret
pursues perfection.
Each measured footfall

is a meditation
in calligraphy.
Each delicate foot
is three *hosofude*,

slender brushes; and
each step is three
brushstrokes, converging
on a common point,

pointing to a past
step towards this step.
The white sand is rice
paper; and the bird

prints it repeatedly,
striving to perfect
its character. Egret—
master of spear,

subject of painting
and poetry—only
calligraphy is
lacking for inner

nobility. Now
it stands on one leg
as if poised, focused
for a final effort—

places with precision
its tri-tufted brush
through the still water.
Lifting up, it leaves,

as if beneath glass,
exquisitely, al-
most excellently,
its pristine figure.

Almost. Such sadness—
to know perfection, yet
never to reach it.
Croaking a regret

it flies to the sun,
the *shodō* egret.

Sacred Kingfisher

If I draw too close
it flies away. Otherwise
it appears not to
notice me at all—the small
kingfisher that comes
to my garden at nightfall
and sets me fishing
for image and metaphor.
It is a brush-stroke
of blue, framed among apples,
famed among feathers.
Still against the shifting leaves,
motionless, it dives
deep into the pools of praise
and surfaces with
itself, conveys nothing else.
It shapes the sprawling
tree by reference to itself:
a lone focal point.
Without knowledge of self, it
enacts itself precisely.

Water Tank

The rain tank by the banana trees:
tap it, follow the corrugations down
until the knuckle's knock
is muffled by water. Climb up,
slide the hatch half-off, find
floating in the blackness
a half-moon full of images:
a tuft of cirrus
fathomed in the tank's troposphere;
the underbelly of a banana leaf
its ribbons fluttering upward
like water-weed; and a face
back-lit, looking back at you.
Unbidden, these blessings of light
long hidden in this dark place.

Poem about Freedom

I am sitting in the shade
of the lemon tree, trying to write
a poem about freedom. But

my son is swinging in the almond,
calling, 'Dad, look at this! Dad!'
The day conspires to distract me

from things I have designated
important. On a branch
arching over me, a lemon's

green rind is yielding to yellow.
Near my feet, a hornet
is hurtling sand from a hole

set in a clear space
between the rootbound and budless
chrysanthemums. In the apple tree

the fruits' round cheeks
are powdered with rouge
and a parrot is summoning its mate

to a feast. Now my daughter
crams her rag doll
in the cane chair beside me and

places in its lap a sprig of mint.
Bruised by her clumsy hands
it smells so clean and sweet.

Distortions

'And when you look through
the smoke, it makes things look funny,
like they shouldn't look,'
said my son, looking through the smoke
of the branches we were burning.

Dugite

The same as with men,
only less dangerously

the snake

where the head goes
the body follows.

Kangaroos Crossing

Emerging from Boongarup Pool
the river flows through
an arbour of casuarinas
then widens to a ford
cobbled with round stones.

On the alluvial flats
beside the broad shallows
I disturbed three kangaroos
from their dozing. Startled,
they fled across the ford,

startling in turn a statue
that broke into a bird.
Now they're gone I see them
again: kangaroos bounding
through the troubled water

and a heron flying up.

Far from Home, the Blower

Close off one end of the didgeridoo
and look down the other—
that's how black he is, this Kimberley man.
He has come to the school for the didgeridoo.
He wants to take it back to his cell,
but I cannot give him permission
immediately. This is a maximum security prison:
procedures must be observed. So
he is playing it now in the literacy room.
I tell the officers he will be staying
for the afternoon. He is playing it now.
His eyes are closed and he is tapping
the plastic seat with his thumbnail
as the pipe drones at his feet.
Abruptly, in a gesture of harmony,
he breaks his rhythm. *That lillgah,*
he says. I do not understand.
Lillgah, he says, slowly, several times.
I cannot get it right. *Lillgah—like tuning.*
Making didgeridoo same as singer.
He plays again. A singer silent to me
is chanting in the channels of his ear.
He listens, trying to match his music
to the key and rhythm of the voice.
We always do this, start
with lillgah. If the singer not happy
with one blower, he get another.
Me a deep blower. He blows again. Indeed
the drone is deep. But I never knew
it could be otherwise. *Some singers are high.*
You know? Clear. He throws his head back,
taps his throat, and sings—high, nasally,
rhythmic, in 'language'.
I know this singing, but its meaning

is ancient and alien. He is singing
and we are in harmony. I do not
ask for meanings. But I say,
Sing low then, Simon. And he sings
low and husky, unlike anything
I have heard before. *The blower*
must be the same. See?
He plays again. A different rhythm.
An officer comes in, jangling
his keys. O freedom! I do not look up.
The didgeridoo drones vibrantly,
striking up a resonance in my soul.
Taut or slack, spiritual chords
are strung across the hollow
at the heart of every man.
No man is mere matter—therefore
the Dreaming. 'Kudda, brother,'
one of the tribal men from Kalgoorlie way
calls me. A man from Noonkanbah Station
greets me behind these walls as 'Papaji,
brother.' Simon does not call me 'brother',
but he is playing the didgeridoo
for me. He breaks off suddenly. *Now*
the young girls come in. Jdirree-jdirree.
He flicks his hands, makes a few staccato
movements with his torso. *Wanga.*
That the Law. The women start first.
He begins again, the familiar droning
tempered by new rhythms and sounds.
And somewhere in the didgeridoo
a brolga begins to dance and cry.
The men this time. First the brolga
dance. He stops again. *Now*
a dingo. She crying for her pup. And
distant through the droning, a dingo
barks and howls in the hollow

of the didgeridoo. *When I was initiated …*
He is rehearsing his life.
And I am a cut and ochred
hollow branch: he speaks into me
evoking a sympathy that, in turn, stirs
his heart to a symphony of longing.
When I am made a man, the blower
he's playing all day. Never stop.
He be giving me his wind.
And they give me a didgeridoo, to be
a blower. But I never play
all day for initiation. I never be picked
to play all night for corroboree.
I only play short time. For fun.
You know? Maybe for white people too.
For fun. Like frogs. Gningi-gningi.
I can't catch the words.
He is sharing unfamiliar things
in a voice too quiet and quick. *A good blower,*
he cut his tongue with spinifex.
He pokes out his tongue. It is very pink
against his purple lips. He runs his thumbnail
down the tip. Yours cut? I ask.
No. Too fat. But good blower,
he listens. He hears. He gets the wisdom of it.
He cuts his tongue, gets plenty sounds.
Plenty wind. Like tortoise. Like crocodile.
You know? His gaze is distant.
He is dreaming. *To be a blower,*
he says, *to be a didgeridoo-man*
is good. You know? Get respect. Get proudness.

Sometimes in the Dark
Bandyup Women's Prison

There is, someone claims,
a pup in the prison.
And then a *yap!* confirms
it. Who now can work?

The women, the inmates,
are excited. The welfare
officer has passed the gates
with a pup at her heels!

It is trotting along
the veranda, towards
H Block—springy, strong
and defiantly doggy.

'Oh!' says one 'girl'
who is serving time
for murder. Memories whirl.
'Oh, I haven't seen a dog

for nearly four years!'
The bars are no barrier
to the pup. It peers
through and the murderess

picks it up and hugs
it with a hard urgency.
It licks her face. No drugs
could put that distance

in her eyes. She thinks,
Four years and six to go.
She shakes her head, blinks
and says for consolation:

'But sometimes in the dark,
far off, I hear them bark.'

In Prison

At least in here,
she said, *he*

can't get at me
or make me do

something
I don't want to.

For Fear of Freedom
Bandyup Women's Prison

She has mutilated, humiliated
herself again, the young woman
soon to be released.

Who can help someone
so lonely, so unlovely?
Everywhere she goes,

everyone ignores her injuries.
As when she defaced her cell
but was not charged,

this self-disfigurement is futile.
For no matter what she does,
they will send her out.

Even here, no one wants her.

Waiting, Singing

She is past eighty and past impatience,
the woman waiting, singing,
by my writing-room window
at the Old Age Centre. She is waiting
for her middle-aged son
who will come, as usual, at his leisure.
And she is singing—sitting on a bench
on the open verandah in the late
mid-winter afternoon—singing—
a tuneless *la-la*-ing
from the shrivelled mouth, the shining heart.
It angers me, his neglect.
Daily, after the Centre is deserted,
she is left waiting, companioned alone
by a voice unmatched to her memories of music.
It disconcerts me, her docility.
So little time left.
Such a waste, just waiting.
Or is it? Perhaps it is glorious
to be singing and not resenting
time going or death coming.

Spring Morning with Baby and Birds

The sun insinuates brightness through the venetian blind.
Why isn't it raining outside? Birds are choking
with song. Why isn't there silence? Our baby
is on her back in the bassinet, blowing spit
onto her chin. She froths at the mouth like a crab
in a bucket. Seeing me, she rubs her heels together,
staccato, quick. Click! Click! 'Go on, little cricket!'
My voice is mechanical, but she smiles just the same.
Her eyes hurt me—so bright with hope. I look away.
She makes a soft sound—the first sound,
apart from crying, of her life—a sort of cooing.
There is a dove in her throat. It becomes in my heart
a bird in a wicker basket. What is this wickedness,
this ingratitude? I place a finger in her palm.
It closes, clasping like a sea anemone.
When she was born, she was embalmed
with vernix. I touched it—a lotion
fit for the thighs of princesses. The old midwives
used to rob the newborn, rub the birth-lotion
on their own bodies. Softer than women, smoother than vernix,
is my daughter's hand. But I am hardened to softness
today. She is trembling with anticipation. But
I do not pick her up—do not
open up to joy. There is a bird in my heart,
fretting. And if it could fly, God would strike it
from the sky. Yet truly, my daughter's smiles,
the spring light, the honeyeaters chirruping
are a burden to me. I prod her.
She coughs out a giggle. In the next room
my older children bicker like politicians.

Lighting a Match

She has learned at last to strike
the red end on the rough edge.
But still they break mid-stroke
or burn her fingers when they burst
to flame. Each match seems to provoke
a failure, invoke from her a cursed
performance. She has begun to learn
what some professors profess to spurn:
From literacy to love to lighting a match,
excellence is the objective ledge
onto which each labour must latch.
No charge of 'elitism' can hedge
this reality from our sight.
For even small things exact a pledge
that we shall do as they would like.

In Transit
for Mike Kelly

Two deaf women are talking on the train,
their dumb speech dancing
from their hands—an astonishing display

of synaesthesia. On this journey
speech has jettisoned me, finger and tongue.
I am too far from home.

Through the window, briefly, a row
of pines—huge, lopsided, limbs hewn back
from the line, trunks studded with stumps.

In the seat facing mine, a young woman
is asleep. Her head droops from her neck
like a cabbage chrysanthemum on a tall stem.

Her face is hidden, but her hands
are translucent-white, and twitch
like spent moths in the cloth of her lap.

The boomgate's thin bell disturbs her
as we race through a crossing. Her neck stiffens,
lifts the lolling head. But her eyes

remain blanketed in their black beds.
Tiredness is a treason in her body
betraying her to sleep among strangers.

Perhaps she is dying. Indeed
this train is death in transit.
One by one, these people will die.

And so will I. I try not to imagine
the accumulated sorrow crammed
into this railcar. We will grieve

those we love because we live
and must die. Why? And what
does deaf or death matter

if we are mere matter? Uprooted
from the pillaged earth, the pines
stand truncated in my mind;

the young woman still droops and dreams;
the dumb women still speak.
We are strangers before You,

hollowed or hallowed by hurt. Father,
the years yield me to yearning
while I tarry in transit to You.

For Grace

Grace is out of grace
for pestering her father.
We are discussing
Important Matters and have
no time for prattle
or play. Grace is out of grace.
Forsaking us, she
clambers onto a carved chest
in the bay-window,
rests her face against the pane,
the crocheted curtains
caped loose across her shoulders.
Outside, a woman
wavers while walking to wave
to a child alone
at a window. Grace's hands
flutter like sparrows
then fall still upon the sill
as the lady leaves.
Even sparrows, Jesus said,
do not fall unseen.
Look then, Father, in the lace
while I pester you for Grace.

Ford

The stones are salmon
shooting the shallows, water
skidding off their backs.

On Haiku

Haiku are pebbles
poets lob into the pond
of our emotions.

Ford and Trees

Below the confluence of Wooroloo Brook and the Swan
several casuarinas stand in the river, their roots

rising compact and conical above the low water.
A chain downstream, the smooth water widens, drops

as from a ledge, along a row of rounded stones, flows
poppled and scarved with foam over the pebbled shallows.

The casuarina trees are the legs of a draughthorse,
their great hooves tufted, flared with root-hairs.

And the starting stones of the ford are the shares
of a plough, blunt blades of dolerite and granite.

Now see how the horse is drawing the plough
upriver, leaving behind the furrowed water.

See too the kangaroos crossing the long paddock,
their elbowed legs sinking in the loose, white loam.

Snake with Angel

When it dived, the dabchick, I ran towards
the swamp, wanting to get closer to see better
before the bird surfaced and saw me—
I sprinted towards the swamp, my eyes
on the black hole in the bright-light-green
weed-covered water where the dabchick had dived—
and running I was not looking at the ground
I was treading and trod within a fraction
of a snake, a tiger snake—big, black-backed
and lightly banded from the orange belly—
by my foot it flicked up,
reared up like a jack jarred from its box,
sprang up and flattened its head
in fear and fury, flattened its face
like a little-hooded cobra charmed
from its basking by the pipe of my leg—
and I staggered off balance like a top
struck while spinning—I stumbled back
expecting through the long seconds
the twin pinholes of poison, oh
expecting—but it teetered, turned, tumbled
down and trickled into the rushes
away from me—and I think, I like to think
an angel, my angel, the angel assigned to me
stepped in to stop the snake from striking me!

Not in Truce

Above the black soil of the bulldozed paddock
spiders have spun their threads
on upraised sticks and roots.
In the midst of anarchy, a small affirmation
of design. The webs,
wet with dew and infused with light,
are white pennants raised to proclaim
the mysterious endurance of the powerless.
Or they are bandages of fine gauze,
daubed where limbs have snapped, wrapped
to staunch the flow of beauty from the broken land.

And perhaps it's only little things that will remain
to shore the heart against the broad and brutal ugliness
that looms as the destiny of man. Perhaps
small gestures—the weaving of poems
or the pursuit of a personal integrity
or an unfaltering faith that God is good and
good is no illusion—are all that is left to us.
Like the spiders, we bind the broken roots.
Not in truce, but on trust, we raise
our ragged, regal flags in the winds of a desolate age.

Waking and Always
Naomi, six months

Where has she gone? I do not hold her
as she sleeps in my arms. The tides of air
lift and let go her chest
with a delicacy that reminds me of death.
So slender, each breath! She is hot
and the sweat glistens like ground glass
on her scalp. Her eyelids are almond petals,
white, exquisitely veined with pink.

Finer than her eyelashes are fine,
yet greater than the delta of the Nile,
are the rivulets of blood in the hoods
of her eyes. The mastery of her!
No human design can hide the design in her.
She holds me as I hold her while she is held
by sleep. Her eyelids flinch and flicker,
brushed by the bright blackness of dreams.

Child, I do not believe your eyelids
or the dreams above which they flutter
are accidental—a mere coincidence
of chemicals and light, a serendipity
of time and matter. I cannot believe.
I lack the faith. Daughter, dream this
true dream: Your spirit is the wick of Yahweh,
your body, the wax of his make and moulding.

Dream this waking and always. And burn,
little candle, burn brightly in the coming night!

from
The Grasshopper Heart
1991

Into Darkness

I am walking at dusk in the lull
between rain. Slugs blot
the footpath. Faintly luminous,
flowers reflect the residual light.

I pass pink, loose-petalled roses,
clumped on bushes like soggy tissues,
and white cabbage chrysanthemums,
battered to the ground and spattered

with sand. I am breaching the border
of twilight, trying not to fear
the fate of my children as they face
the frontier. Like the planet,

my thoughts spin nightward. Retreating,
the day destroys the third dimension,
deprives the world of depth.
Trees turn black. In silhouette

a spindly eucalypt sculptures the rain,
its slender leaves flouncing
in squalls in the hesitant wind.
Through radiating tiers of branches

a Norfolk Island pine points the way
to heaven, holds highmost a cross.
I am walking into darkness. Colours
are draining away, shapes dissolving.

All the old certainties are lost.
Above, the moon is a spillage of light
mopped up by the clouds. The moon
with its meaning: the sun that shone

is still shining. I am walking
through the dark on the turning world.

For the Blind

Sight is not the only sense
to make sense of wattles. Touch

is another. Feel the pods.
They are sentences in Braille,

ribbons of calligraphy
for the fingers of the blind.

Human Rights Poem for Christmas

Murder? I resent the implication!
It's hardly human. Take it from me—
all you see is blood. Get rid of it now.
Who would be the poorer?

Mary, I frankly don't believe
that angel-announcement stuff.
Nor will anyone else. Everyone
knows there's only one way …

All right, calm down! The thing is,
you're not married. Think of the shame
once you begin to show. And Joseph …
do you think he'll still want you?

Think of yourself, your future.
And think—they could stone you.
Then it would die anyway. Besides,
what sort of life will the little …?

Okay, Miss Still-a-Virgin, get off
your Son-of-the-Most-High horse!
I'm just trying to help. One day
you'll regret not listening to reason.

Golgotha

Finally, one arrives at the place
of the skull because there is nowhere
else to go. And there before the face
of bone one pauses in despair.

The culmination of all evil
is displayed before one's eyes.
Man's heart conspired with the devil
and cared little for disguise.

Yet if, at the sight of the Cross,
a light is struck on the rough of the brain
and the mind conceives all bar this is vain,

there comes a voice that reassures: Thus
is the seed of tenderness sown
in the cleft of the heart of stone.

White Gum

This white-barked wandoo,
this most-Australian gum,
rises through the air, rigid
with wood, latent with post

and cross-beam. It is fitting,
really, that this eucalypt,
this kinstree to the Cross
of the Son of God, should be

an incarnation of the light
of the sun—the same sun
the world over, the millennia
long. Run your hand up the trunk

towards the limbs you cannot
reach. There are no splinters
in the bark. Go ahead, touch
the wood, the living timber

the nails have yet to pierce.

Bread

In the beginning God
made grain so that men
might make bread

so that every loaf
might proclaim
its Archetype,

the Living Bread
come down from heaven.
Give thanks and eat!

Marri with Nuts

After rain
sometimes gumnuts
—the big-bowled,

boldly-rimmed
nuts of the marri
—smoulder

as if packed
with tobacco
and set alight.

Or, which is
more beautiful,
as if each nut

were a thurible,
a wooden censer,
wafting incense.

Indeed, this
green-robed tree
is a thurifer

unconsciously
praising God
most consciously

through me.

Communion
for Iain & Liz Parker

The garden is dry but the birdbath
brims with black water from the bottom
of the dam. Beside the gravel path

two stumps beckon small birds from the bush,
invite with a voice they never had
when fused, infused with the sap's green push.

One, on its plane, bears sugar and grain.
The other, in a glazed clay dish, holds
the dark dregs of last winter's light rain.

A neat, white-naped honeyeater takes
a bath. A fantail alights to flirt.
On the flat grass nearby, like snowflakes,

a fall of rolled oats. Be still. Don't speak.
Share this communion: a blue wren is
breaking a white wafer with his beak.

Leaf and Load

The rain is breaking its phials
on the ornamental plum. From
the veranda I choose a leaf,

glistening with wet, and watch
until each vein becomes a rill
running into the midrib-river

and on to the leaf's tip
where the waters gather in a blister
to weight the leaf downwards

by imperceptible degrees. Slipping
from the chlorophyll plane, the rain-
drop hangs from the leaf-tip

as a ball-bearing might hang
from the point of a magnet, held
by the barest contact between

curve and cusp. Like a miniature
transparent balloon tied by a child
to a tap, the drop swells,

bulges with a fragile elasticity,
bowing the leaf with its growing load,
until loosed at last by gravity.

Released, the leaf leaps up,
shudders to an easy equilibrium
in the light, impacting rain.

The Grasshopper Heart

That man with the cowboy hat and tan and tattoos
is holding his little white-skinned daughter
very gently in the shallow water. Now he is
zooming her along, but not too quickly
for fear of her fear. He tosses her up,
catches and hugs her, holds in check
the fierce tenderness that craves to crush her.
Her father. His wholly holy love. He is smiling
and I know his heart is like a grasshopper—
leaping and landing spring-loaded to leap again.

Spring, Alfred Cove

This wildlife sanctuary: the last wetland on the Swan
River estuary. How long will it last? Some call it
wasteland, and few notice it at all. A patch of sedge

signals in semaphore to an inattentive world.
Samphires mat the mudflats, their bulbous stems
like strings of red and green rosary beads. Bulrushes

grow on a bank, their cylindrical bales of wool
bursting open from the season's rough, ripe handling.
With its numerous, invisible needles, the wind

knits the water plain and purled. Pelicans,
their wings unfurled, float fathoms above the cove,
caught in slow, wide eddies. Terns in turn

kamikaze the battleship-grey water, rise again
unhurt. A dozen black ducks at the water's edge
quack quietly as they dredge the sludge. Stilts

step on their reflections with their spindly,
backward-bending legs. Cormorants practise Tai Chi
on wireless and weathered fence posts. An egret

stands without a mate beside a beached boat.
Also alone, a greenshank hunts along the sandbars.
Soon others will come from Siberia,

charting their course by the changeless stars.

from
Between Glances
1993

The Visitor
for Nicholas

My landlord's small, blond-haired boy
comes daily to peer through my windows—
four oblongs of glass forming the corner
of the room against which my writing desk
is nestled. My sunpanels and pleasures.

Disadvantaged by the light, he presses
his pale face to a pane and cups his hands
about his eyes, trying to gaze in at me
without glare. Yes, his eyes confirm,
the man is there, sitting still as always.

Often he startles me, having approached
on his bare feet as quietly as a cat
on its paws. He stares in now, the glass
glazing with his breath. I glance at him
and smile. But only briefly, hoping

neither to encourage nor discourage him.
For after all, I have come to this room
wanting not visitors but visitations.
And he seems perfectly to understand.
He watches quietly for a moment then

leaves. Today, out of sweet courtesy,
he returned, touched the window, and said,
'I'm going now.' I smiled and nodded,
and wondered if I ought to press my palm
to the glass, as I have seen prisoners do

before their loved ones leave the visiting
room and the gaol to go free in the world.

Between Glances

It is a liquidambar, the tree
I planted two months ago
beside my study. Green and
leafy then, it is almost bare

now. A little twiggy thing.
One red leaf flutters from it
like a child's hand. For a week
it has been waving to me,

wanting my attention, trying
to tell me something unknown
to eucalypts and evergreens.
Something European or Japanese.

Something sad and deciduous.
That brave beautiful leaf,
beckoning the eyes as a flame
beckons the palms. All day

it has warmed me. Exquisite,
that small wind-chafed hand,
its familiar flutter. I glance
down at my work then out

again, only to find it gone.
Gone between glances. If only
I had known that last wave
was a goodbye, a farewell,

I would not have looked away.

Birthday

It is my birthday
and my daughter, who doesn't
suspect the sadness
of a spent year, comes prancing
before her mother
into my cluttered workroom
clutching a present.
I rip the wrapping to find
a small scribble pad
upon which she's proudly drawn
a pony with black
spots on its back and a red
smear on its muzzle.
'What is the red?' 'That's lipstick,'
she says. I wonder
why, but do not ask. The horse
with red lipstick stands
in a field of yellow grass
beneath a blue sky—
just glad to be alive, glad
to see me with its green eye.

Wine Country

Playtime and the children
are charged with games
and loud alliances.

Beside the school the vines
have linked arms
among the rowdy dandelions.

Sunshower

The sun is shining yet rain
is falling. Light rain,
like splinters of light,
floating down. Straight down,

no wind to waft it about.
Looking at the trees is like
looking through a faintly
scratched sheet of Perspex.

Two children, not mine,
are running through the forest.

Sonnet of Thanksgiving

I wake, draw the curtains and am suddenly aware
that he is profligate, our God, giving us more
than we need, more than we ever dream to ask for.
Through the window on this winter morning, there

beside my house, the forest is faint with mist.
The white trees are like women standing half-seen
in a sauna. The bushes where the spiders have been
are strewn with ornaments for throat and wrist:

necklaces, bracelets, strung with diamonds. A stark
and startling wealth, this jewellery the women
have put off. They stand in silent communion:
unadorned, white, bar the occasional birthmark.

And then in the stillness, the whiteness, the swirl,
a lone bird call: it hangs on the ear like a pearl.

Rhyme

I sing a rhyme for my daughter
of a teapot short and stout.
She mimes a clumsy kettle,
crooks a handle, points a spout.

The world is wide with danger,
my life is dark with doubt,
but a child commands me sweetly,
'Come on, Daddy, dance and shout!'

Sometimes I sense my children
have turned my life about.
They top me up with gladness,
tip me over, pour me out.

Mirth with Meaning

After the meal, we read
the words of Christ in the Gospel
of Matthew: 'When you fast,
do not look dismal …'

'What does 'fast' mean?' I ask.
My daughter jumps from her chair
and races around the table.
'See—I'm fast!' she declares.

Who dares laugh? Angels
rollick about the room. I nod
earnestly. There is a smile
on the three Faces of God.

Grace

It is the genuflexion of the head,
whether tonsured or permed,
that believers have thrice-daily
in common. A communion of thanksgiving.

'For what we are about to receive …'
So easy to make of it a mockery
or a cliché. And yet these words,
or the gist of them, hold a real if ritual
gratitude. Or a sadness at the discrepancy
between what is and what ought to be.
'… Lord, make us truly thankful.'

Monks in the refectory, mothers
in the kitchen, give thanks before
the first mouthful of every meal.

In the labour and re-education camps
maimed men and wasted women
murmur without a mutter before
guzzling their gruel. In the black lands
where droughts and dictators conspire
against the belly, believers still
say the blessing as they apportion
the last cup of begged grain.

Others, in the wonderworld of the West,
are flustered as they bow at their feasts
by memories of the dreams of Joseph:
the lean cows eating up the sleek ones—
the famished beasts rising from the river
dripping and treading down the reeds
and eating their kind, their kith and kine,
like cannibals. The bellows. The blood

on the bovine teeth. And the second dream
of the seven fat ears of wheat
swallowed up by the seven skinny. Horrible,
the blighted grain gaping ravenously.
A nightmare. Let those who have ears hear.

Yet without ears, he hears.
Our infinite, intimate God leans to listen
to the myriad momentary prayers
of his people. Saying grace. It is our incense.
It is, beyond explanation, his satisfaction.

'Let us give thanks.' And millions
at mealtimes do. Even infants,
those most insouciant of souls,
offer thanksgiving with cries and cooing
as they nuzzle at the breast—
that guzzle-and-come-again fount
where form and feast fuse in bliss
and soft blessing. See how they tug
away from the nipple, smiling.

Eyes closed and heads bowed: it is
the only way to look up. Thank
You. And think of it, the dignity
we gain through humility. Being
grateful. Giving thanks. That precious
repetitious prayer that makes us remember
grace as we say it.

This Abundance

The thing that astonishes me is that
life goes on abundantly without me.
Stepping out of my study, I discover
magpies have made a nest not twenty
metres from the house. By the gate

the buds of the *Eucalyptus preissiana*
are a hatching of chickens: a yellow
fuzz beneath the raised opercula.
A small girl skips along the road,
her hair in a pony tail, flouncing.

A neighbour hails me for a yarn.
'Yes,' he says. 'This old bloke lived
in a thousand gallon tank at Kulikup
and cut sleepers with an adze.'
His memory is almost twice my age.

As we talk, his dog paws at a puddle
in the gravel, then pokes its muzzle
into the muddy water—sticks its face
in right up to its ears! Fancy that!
Fancy a dog doing that—and me there

to see it! Truly, it's an astonishment,
this abundance independent of me
that touches me seemingly by accident.

Kangaroos

Silent as the light-
ly falling rain,
kangaroos are bounding
in single file
across the near paddock.

A buck, a doe, a joey,
diminishing in size
like a trick
of perspective, going
fast, their tails

working up and down
like the handle of a pump,
spring-loading
their legs for each jump.
Without pause, the buck

leaps the fence
but the smaller two balk
at the last moment.
Now, without momentum,
they are without hope

of hurdling the wire.
They race along the fence,
the curve of their down-
swinging tails touching
the angle of their up-

springing heels. It is
no use. The barrier
is unbroken. Finally
they stop, stand still
and stare into the bush.

Two grey skittle-shapes,
thalidomide paws
clasped to their chests.
Bewildered, they gaze back
across the open paddock

to where a rainbow has
raised a bright crosier
to bless the dreadful world.

Happiness

A small green bird is hopping
up the grey trunk of a river gum.
The tree leans toward the water.
A duck floats on its reflection.

The climbing bird knocks a fleck
of bark into the water. The duck
inspects it then paddles away.
The Chinese poet Tu Fu wrote,

'After the laws of their being
all creatures pursue happiness.'
Watching the birds, the dragon-
flies, it occurs to me that Fu

is quite wrong. Apart from man,
all creatures simply *are* happy.
No duck ends the day with regret.
We alone aspire to something

Other. And we alone fall short.

Courtyard

In the courtyard of
the pottery, mauve petals
float upon the rain
water in the blue-glazed bowl
from which the cat is lapping.

Tea with Susan

I am sipping tea
with my wife in the shade of
a white magnolia.
A single petal has fallen
onto my book of Chinese poems.

Reaction to a Retard

Disgusting, really, the way it disfigures
the face—a lack of intelligence. The 'retard'
on the ferry has nothing going for him
except his mother, who gives him a regard

I struggle to comprehend. I hear a quick
voice cry, *Better to kill him before birth!*
I look at him and shudder at my own depravity.
How easy it is to deny a person worth—

to limit the human, which is the image
of God, to the beautiful and clever,
and to forget there is in every person
a spark, a spirit, that abides for ever.

There is a worse disorder than the damaged
brain that disfigures the blameless face.
It is the derangement of the cogent mind
that deforms the heart by a denial of grace.

from
Fontanelle
2004

The Sleep of the Upright

A man snared
by slumber

in a chair
in the library

has assumed
the pose of

a swan asleep—
neck curved,

head aslant
and down.

A gawky grace,
yet strangely moving—

for he looks
so vulnerable

without a wing
to cover his face.

Impression

This could be Egypt, they could be gods:
three white ibises standing on a sandbar.
One preens its plumes, another peers
along the river, while the third steps
to the shallows to probe among the lilies.
This is not the Nile. There are no gods
but God. Yet how striking the impression:
this could be Egypt, they could be gods!

Apples
for Susan

She lifts her long skirt
to cradle the windfalls.
Her legs are very white,
like the flesh of apples.

Some things about women
a woman can never know.
Else she would not stand
with her skirt caught up.

Or she would more often.
She stands in the shade
of the laden tree, unaware
I am aware of her legs.

Beloved, even the apples
are blushing in your lap.

Conception

Child, some things you cannot,
and others you should not,
know. But I want you to know
this about your beginning:

Within days of my sending,
by love and desire, half
of possible-you in search
of your possible other half,

she said, my wife your mother,
'My breasts are tender.' So
we suspected the possible
had become actual in her.

Then finally she confirmed
your presence by the absence
of blood. Pregnant! Oh, baby,
how becomingly you became!

And be assured we were glad.
We felt things past measure.
Oh, we thought, felt. *Ah,
such wonder from our pleasure!*

Opulence

Her milk has come in
but our son still sleeps.

I cup my palm. Oh,
such a hard opulence!

She lies awake, willing
his hot mouth to squall.

My heart aches with love
as a breast with milk.

Fontanelle

Strange, this seeing
the heart in the head.

Look, a drumming
in the cranium,

a tom-tomming
against the membrane

where the bones are
yet to meet and knit.

May they never
knit entirely, son.

May head and heart
beat in unison

always, as now
in your fontanelle.

The Weight of the Baby
Marroning, Wellington Weir

I stay behind with the baby
while they check the baits—
my wife, my children. They are
that light skirting the shore.

My new son lounges in my arms,
staring at my face, which is
(like his own but less sweetly)
uneven with shadow and shine.

Gas hisses in the lamp's gauze.
A sudden wind scours the weir
like a scoop net. Behind me,
the trees break out in tongues.

Sensing the soft grasp of sleep,
the child begins to struggle,
limbs erratic and ineffectual
as a marron marooned on its back.

'Don't be cross,' I murmur,
hugging him, rocking him. 'Hush.'
I am gentled from my gender,
staying back with the baby.

He settles and slips away.
His head becomes heavy,
like a melon, in the crook
of my arm. Light meshes

in his hair as if in a mantle.
Distant but distinct, I hear
my eldest son scoop and exclaim.
A scrabble of claws on wire.

The water is black but the sky
is spattered with stars.
I imagine the many rubies
of the marron's torchlit eyes.

I watch my family, my loves,
move further into the darkness.
A mopoke cries from the forest.
I feel the weight of the baby.

I feel the weight but am light.
O Lord, my soul is very still,
quiet and still, even as an infant
asleep in his father's arms.

Homecoming

It is thrilling to be so loved.
Hearing my step on the veranda
he bellows to Mum that I'm home
and races to the door to greet me.

To be so loved. It is thrilling.
Seeing me he bursts into welcome,
with glad prattle, great prancing
and that sheer shine on his face!

A Thing or Two about Monkeys

'There's no monkey in the shower,
see?' He is reluctant to look.
At two he's old enough to know
a thing or two about monkeys.

And there *is* one in the shower—
dangling, perhaps, from the nozzle,
waiting to drop on his head to
join the one causing the trouble.

But where did *that* one come from?
What word or image summoned it
to swing with grimace and gibber
through the synapses of his brain?

And how astonishing that it
could come at all! Can a monkey
imagine a boy in the shower?
So how then a boy, a monkey?

He peers into the tiled recess.
Is that a face behind the wash
cloth on the tap? Is that a paw
clasping the curtain to the rail?

He concedes at last his mistake.
But soon he begins to wonder,
Which rooms in the house are safe
now the monkey's left the shower?

Mowing

I turn to see my son behind me.
He pauses as I pause, a few paces
back in the swath in the weeds.

When did he leave the veranda?
When did he resolve the mower's roar
would no longer make him scream?

As I move off he comes on, ginger
as a cat. He is stalking his fear.
Come on, then, little one. Be brave.

Two isn't too young to rehearse.
Courage is hard, cowardice easy.
And fear … fear gets only worse.

Shock

I was writing about dragons
when a bird mistook glass for air.
The shock of it, that whack
against the window! The bird
fell. The dragons fled.
I stepped out to the veranda
to find a cuckoo gasping
by the wall. A bronze cuckoo,
too hurt to be afraid of my hand.

Lacking a mageword for healing,
a wardword for death,
I dissolved a pinch of sugar
in a teaspoon, dripped
a drop in the back of its throat.
It began to choke, beak agape,
tongue thrusting like a dagger.
Then it grew calm. And I
grew amazed. Astonished at
the wild thing in my palm,
the clarity of glass,
the collision of the two,
the coincidence of my presence.

I placed it back at last
on the veranda in the sun.
Winter sun just warm enough
for a bird in shock to bask in.
And as I kept watch from my desk,
the dragons came back,
came back in a hoard. I invoked
warriors with bow and sword
to divert them away from the bird.

Home
for Susan

The night is coming on fast now.
Looking out the window I see
the forest on the far hill
has become a mass of blackness
with frills against the skyline.
The kangaroos in the near paddock
have blurred into the pasture.
The irrigation dam down in the valley
glistens silver-grey, a scrap
of twilight torn from the sky.
The words I've been working with
are like running water. All afternoon
I've been trying to scoop out
a place for them to settle, a poem
where they can lie and reflect the light.
But it's too late now. The dark
is coming on fast, fast. And I want
to go home. My wife is expecting me.
She is in the kitchen right now
making tea, with the two little ones
tripping her up, climbing
over each other like ferrets.
She is waiting to ask me, 'How
did it go?' And I will say, 'Good.'
Or, 'Not so good.' Depending.
And she will kiss me, just a touch
of her lips to my lips, but
a touch nonetheless. And my sons,
with four years of life between them,
will bully me for attention.
And I will toss them about,
roughing them up with love.
And later tonight, before we join

the children in that no-place
of sleep, she might embrace me.
Or she might not. Either way
is fine. Tomorrow will be different.
Only her constancy is constant.
Two decades ago she vowed,
'With my body, my heart, my will,
I will.' And truly she has, does.
Amazing! My wife. She's the one,
she's the one I'm going home to now.
Home. The place she makes
by being there. The place
that resolves the question, 'Who,
who in this life will love me?'

White Ibis

It is luminous,
the ibis standing
on the shimmer
of its reflection
in the autumn light.

The water lilies
defer to it.
The breeze touches
reverently the hem
of its garment.

Spreading its wings,
it adorns the sky
as a seraph
adorns with adoration
the eternal heavens.

Breaking free from
the departing bird,
a single feather
shies and spins
in the wings' wake.

Alighting, the plume
lies like foam
on the restless
water, a token
of something numinous.

Rose

The day after I cut it
I notice the white rose
in the pottery vase
on my desk start to wilt.

All day it has been
drooping lower and lower,
until now its small head
is hanging upside down,

lolling loose-haired
against the shoulder
of the vase, as if given
entirely to sorrow.

He Knows a Place

He knows a place we cannot share,
a wholly black and boundless space,
and when he went he drew us there.

It is the rift left in a tear,
a bullet or a blade's wet trace,
this place he knows we cannot share.

It is the darkness called despair
that none survive except by grace.
And when he went he drew us there.

Don't go, beloved! Oh, beware!
Don't turn your heart and set your face
upon that place we cannot share!

Sorrow and sickness were the fare
that gave him passage to that place.
And when he went he drew us there.

It barely counts how much we care.
This is the fact we must embrace:
he knows a place we cannot share,
and when he went he drew us there.

Pathos

There is no bound to a father's
suffering and love. Ask our Father.

Ask mine. See how gently he is
tilting my brother's wounded head

to shave the stubble from his jaw.

Listening to Louis

Though he is dead, Louis Armstrong
rasps out, 'What a wonderful world!'

then shifts into a slow rendition of
'Nobody knows the trouble I've seen.'

Just how true these words are, and
sad as true, 'Nobody knows but Jesus.'

Journey

Because the journey
was his destination
he was always and never

where he wanted to be,
the haiku master,
Matsuo Bashō,

who set out from Edo
in the spring of 1689
on *The Narrow Road*

to the Deep North.
Now 300 years later
he has set out again,

travelling in translation:
my mind his staff,
my heart his companion.

Christmas Tree

Gold was among the gifts
that the wise men brought to Jesus.
(See how the tall one lifts

the sack from his saddle
and pours the coins into the lap
of Mary by the cradle?)

Gold is a gift for kings;
but wise men aren't the only ones
who understand such things.

For on the western side
of Australia, a peculiar tree
fills the bush with pride

each Christmas, with a bold
and brilliant display of blossoms
as bright as molten gold.

Rejoice! Even the odd,
the unlovely and misshapen
may offer gifts to God!

Christmas trees are ugly
trees. Their leaves are tatty and dull
and their limbs are straggly.

Their wood's a carpenter's loss,
being too weak to bear the weight
of a rafter or a cross.

And yet on Christmas Day,
between banksias and eucalypts,
by roads and in paddocks, they

blaze with a beauty that hurts
the eye. (See them fling their nuggets
into the sky's blue skirts!)

Nuytsia floribunda:
a little tree with gifts of gold
on the Day of Wonder!

Parable
for Leroy Randall

Plant a seed, reap a song:
such are the ways of God.

Jesus said his kingdom
is like a mustard seed

which when buried rises
to a tree, and the birds

alight in its branches.
So, from a grain, a surge

of sap and shade, a haunt
of gladness and surprise.

Oh, beyond all desire,
the tree of God abounds

with nests—and a choir!

Painting in the Painting
Margaret Olley's oil on canvas, Girl sewing

Is it to fill a space on the wall
or in the girl, that painting
in the painting of a *Girl sewing*?

See it? Above her bowed head,
a small bluish square with black slap-
dash strokes coalescing as boats.

Prow, gunnel, mast—three vessels.
Onboard one, I suspect, a boy,
trawling the heart of the sewing girl.

Drawing a thread through her cloth,
she imagines a line in the creases
of his fingers. 'Oh, Johnny, John!'

she murmurs. 'Let me be your sea.
I have waves and a harbour. Oh,
come back, and be a mariner to me!'

Woman Weeping, Sydney

Because she is sitting side-on to me,
I can see she has been crying, the woman
wearing mirrored glasses in the café.

Pity the animals, that they cannot weep.
Pity us, that we can, must, so often.
Her boyfriend returns with ice coffees.

She glances at him with her hidden eyes.
Her face crumples a little, sucked in
by the vacuum of her grief. He offers

a paper napkin, and she dabs her eyes,
shunting her sunglasses up the bridge
of her nose. Then she clears the mucus.

He looks away as one looks away from
something unpleasant. Shoring her face
with an unsure smile, she sips her coffee,

her larynx almost jamming in her throat.
He takes a tourist map from his backpack,
lays it between them, studies the streets.

She parts her thin lips, making a path
to her lungs for the persistent air.
She says something to him. Foreign words.

What is the meaning? Why is she crying?
Has he hurt her? Is she ill? Homesick?
Surely, she is far from home. Very far.

We all are. Only most of us don't know it.

Should the Marauders Come

She won't go back to the farm
while her husband is in hospital.
She can't go back. She's afraid
of being afraid out there
by herself at night, out there
with only the ducks and the calves
to hear her screech (oh horror,
horror!) should the marauders come.

And who's to say they won't come
for her as they came for that man
at Manjimup? Three teenagers
at the farmhouse door with hearts
like fists, fists with knives.
Three robbers who stopped short
of murder because they thought
the stabbed man was stabbed dead.

One in a million, of course. But
who's to say that of the next million
she's not the next one? Besides,
another marauder is waiting already.
Those empty boots, that unwrinkled
sheet! *My beloved!* The presence
of his absence is stalking through
the house. She knows it, knows it!

Don't try to counsel or correct her.
She is right to be afraid
of being afraid out there alone.
Let her stay in town at the motel.
There are noises there to remind her
she is not alone in the world.
And people nearby who will hear,
perhaps even help, if she should scream.

Gladdened by Ibises

As unexpected as the first sighting,
this remembrance of those ibises.
By-passing my retina, they enter
my brain, shimmer like mirages
in the blackness of my skull.
A pair of sacred ibises, white-
bodied, black-necked and -tailed.
Standing knee-deep in the kikuyu
on the river bank in the park,
they preen themselves awkwardly
with their long curved beaks.
Sicklebirds. One turns its bill sideways
to scissor its breast feathers,
while the other bends its neck
to probe the plumage between its legs.
Inexplicably, I see them as I saw them.

And it occurs to me that those birds
are somewhere out there still,
still being ibises, still doing
ibisy things. Impervious to me,
they occupy the same time as me
but move in a different space.
Where, I wonder? What swamp, creek
or weir? Perhaps they never left
the park. Or have returned. Yes.
Surely they are in the park now
with someone about to see them!
Someone I don't know. A woman,
perhaps. A middle-aged woman who,
being a little chunky and melancholy,
is out walking to lift the weight
from her hips, her heart.

Glancing up she sees them, the same
ibises I saw, the very pair I see
in the virtual reality of my head!
And she thinks, *Oh, a white bird
with a black bustle! Two of them.*
And she stands for a moment, simply
gladdened by ibises. The nearest one
twists its liquorice-stick neck
to settle a feather on its shoulder.
Then suddenly alarmed, it croaks
and takes to the clear cold air,
its companion following close.
And she watches them go, this woman
whose life my life has never touched,
watches those sacred ibises wing
along the glossy water and round

the river bend. And when at last
she moves on she hardly feels
any weight at all. She could almost
skip, skip like her granddaughter,
as she walks with those white birds
spreading their wings in her mind.

Boat

The new boat. I bought it mostly
for my boy, who at fifteen has become
black and thunderous. An aluminium
dinghy with ten horses behind it—
something to interest him, something
to give us something in common.
And yesterday it did. I swear
he was almost happy as we launched
the boat in the bay for the first time.
Our small craft. At full throttle
it sat up and planed! A sensation
of speed, as in a go-kart! Today
he wants to try it by himself.
Sure, I say, stepping to the shore.
Why not? I push the prow out to sea.
He pulls the cord and powers away,
heads out without looking back.
The dinghy skips over the light chop,
going out and out. I watch him,
the boy I've not loved nearly enough.
My son, who grows bigger in my heart
even as he grows smaller in my eyes.
He is on the sea, going directly
away from me. And I notice now
what I should have noticed before—
the cloudbank on the horizon.
Black clouds coming in. And the boy
still going out! I watch and watch,
willing him to turn. The boat
no longer glints, having gone
into the shadow of the clouds.
Then suddenly a tear, a bright tear
in the fast encroaching blackness.
And another. No thunder. No rain.

Just lightning, synapsing the dark sky
to the dark sea! The level sea,
on which my son is the highest point.
The empty sea, on which our boat
is the only boat. Lightning! Oh son,
turn back, turn back to the shore!
I beckon and call. But he has gone
too far to see or hear me any more.

from
Birds in Mind:
Australian nature poems
2009

Brimming

A cup on a cross-
beam in the carport,

a grass cup covered
with a cobweb gauze—

the nest some goodness
has filled to the brim

with wagtail hatchlings
that lift wobbling heads

above the low rim
and gape with gladness

each time their parents
return with insects,

not to mention twit-
chings and chitterings!

Birds Bathing

Despite winter chills—
robins at their ablutions
in a reddish dish
on a stump beside a small
bare tree ringed by daffodils.

Each Lily

Each arum lily
beside the dam's amphitheatre
is holding aloft
(as at carols by candlelight)
a yellow flame in a white cup.

Sighting
On visiting the Bull Ranges with a traditional landowner.

Pluck out the detecting eye,
break off the pointing finger,
shut up the exclaiming cry—
if only somehow I could!

But it's too late to stifle
myself now or stop my friend,
who snatches up his rifle
and follows swiftly after

the wallabies I sighted,
the small wild rock wallabies
whose survival I blighted
simply because I saw them

and cried aloud, delighted.

Menace

It's not just the colours,
the burnt-out blacks and blazing oranges

It's not just the flying,
the buzzing wings and erratic barging

It's also the walking,
the stop-starting and upstart dart-poking

With all the while the wings
rigid and out-jutting from the thorax …

Yes, above all, the wings,
those at-the-ready wind-whetted switchblades

Wings angled like the arms
of a bad man, a madman, hands on hips

Elbows crooked defiant,
daring any hothead to take him on—

The spider-hunting wasp
roving on and around the garden rocks

Black Cockatoos

As they like all creatures
came originally from Mind,
not matter, the cockatoos
are part of the supernatural.

And hearing a large flock
croak and snarl and creak
in the crowns of the gums,
I realise just how easily

a man could mistake them
for black spirits, demented
and dreadful, if he did not
know that 'black' as a state

of the heart belongs sadly
solely to humans and demons.

Irises

      i

The grey water tank—
how vividly it sets off
the mauve irises!

      ii

Purple irises …
I rather prefer the ones
that Vincent painted.

Croaking

      i

On the second beat
a second frog also croaks—
chill winter evening.

      ii

Antiphonal—
two frogs calling either end
of the puddle.

Fitting

      i

A hermit crab—
beachcombing at low tide for
a fitting shell.

      ii

A little cramped—
the seashell the hermit crab
tries on for size.

      iii

Remarkable—
a hermit crab has restored
life to a shell!

Birds in Mind

     i

Sacred kingfisher—
into the world onto the branch
courtesy the King.

     ii

Wren and the art
of bird-making—dear Lord, such
blue in the bush!

     iii

Statuesque heron—
unmoved as humans debate
the Sculptor question.

     iv

Goodness, that ibis
signals the presence of birds
in the mind of God!

from
Far from Home:
Poems of faith, grief and gladness
2010

Healing

    I

There comes a time when longing fills the soul.
Shapes lose their power on the mind
and to the bright of colour the eye is blind.
Strangely, without warning, we are no longer whole
and all things are gone beyond our control.
In the subtlety of sound the ear can find
no euphony; and the heart, inclined
to sadness, in everything finds nothing to extol.

It is as if too long and too far from home
we have journeyed without thinking
of arrival—and standing finally alone
at the water's edge with the last light winking,
we find all things tinged with tragedy,
like the sun sinking down to the sea.

    II

The sun sinking down to the sea,
magenta and majestic in his splendour,
appears powerless to prevent the plunder
of night. *Rise up! Look on us and let us see!*
But he is gone. Will he ever again be free?
He stood for a moment on the water
then was swallowed up, seemingly forever.
Who are we to have seen this? Oh, who are we?

Yet still we stand in the darkness waiting
for something to happen, for something more.
The moon is ill and the stars fall fainting
while the waves wash muted on our shore.
The brush of night tars the troubled air
and the heart's longing turns to despair.

III

The heart's longing turns to despair
and all seems dark and death within.
Yet in the din of defeat the voice of victory rings,
peals out the promise of our Creator's care.
There begins in our being the flare
of dawn: the Sun rising with healing in his wings.
With the gold of his blood he spins
fine silk, weaves a mantle for the faint to wear.

All things again are new and bright,
from the great to the least, the comely to the plain,
each in its own way is clothed with light.
In passing loss is permanent gain.
Hence, that if it will it might be whole,
there comes a time when longing fills the soul.

Hurt

A woman singing
Mississippi John Hurt blues …
She croons his ballad
about angels, death and dirt,
laying me away with hurt.

Fathers

Over the air waves,
weeping, a father whose son
killed by negligence
another father's daughter …
Oh, Father—justice, mercy!

You Gladly
for Susan

'The curves of your thighs
are like jewels, the work
of a skilled craftsman.' Who

did Solomon have in mind?
Dearest, I have you only,
you gladly, in mind. Re-

mind me again, won't you?
Allure me with the lines
and limber of your limbs.

As on our wedding night,
the first of all nights,
let me please the Craftsman

with my pleasure in you.

The Worship Tanka

1
Psalm

The congregation,
singing David's ancient poem
to the mellow sound
of my daughter's saxophone:
so my soul longs after You ...

2
Benediction

For benediction
I raise my hand and the people
bow their heads—except
a small boy, who raises *his* hand
to bestow a blessing on *me!*

3
After Preaching

Thanking me warmly
for my sermon, an old woman—
'I couldn't hear it
myself, I'm nearly deaf, but
everyone said it was lovely.'

Path

If we look we see
the Son's light like the sun's light
makes a straight path
across the sea to each of us
wherever we stand on the shore.

Use

It is no excuse
and yet our sin has this use:
the Father of Lights
in the dark of our disgrace
shows the glory of his grace.

Bravery

When I face the grave
Jesus will not deplore me
if I am not brave.
After all, it was hardly
a strong man he came to save.

Dignity

To be dignified
when facing death is mainly
a matter of pride.
What matters most is to trust
the One who was crucified.

The God of the Glimpses
7 poems from a sequence of 32 poems on the Prophet Elijah
(1 Kings 16:28-18:11)

By My Word
Elijah

When Yahweh judges a nation,
even the righteous are reviled.
I do not know when it began but
one day I noticed—above my camp
where the water hung like a banner
over the balcony of stone—
a diminution. And downstream,
on a flat rock in the brook's bed,
on either side of the trickling
current, I saw a black crust on a stone
where once there had been slime
beneath a film of flowing water.
Then I realised, as if it were
a great revelation, that the brook
was drying. The source of my life
was failing due to the drought
I had summoned by God's word
and could dismiss by mine. I watched
closely now and each day I saw
the stream narrow and the black,
crusty border widen. The frogs

stopped croaking. The small fish
no longer faced into the current
but circled aimlessly, penned
in small pools. I remembered the rock
Moses struck for water in the wilderness
and begged, 'Which rock, Lord,
shall I strike?' The white heron
shook its priestly plumage and
flew away. Finally, the ravens failed
to return. And still no word,
no whisper. But there was not silence.
I heard a voice that said, 'No rain
except by my word.' *My* word!
I heard it again and again, until
I knelt and prayed for strength
not to pray for rain.

Two Things Unclean
Elijah

On the third day of thirst his voice came: 'Go
to Zarephath. A widow there will feed you.'
But I protested, 'Lord, it is a town
of Sidon of the Phoenicians. It is beyond
the borders of Israel, among the gentiles.
Are there not many widows in Israel, Lord?
Is none worthy to succour your servant?
First the ravens, now the pagans.
Lord, is there nothing holy for my help?'

Behind the Glimpses
The widow

Since my husband died, I have been seeking
a saviour. Someone unlike Baal, who,
if his priests are true, is bloody and brutal.
And someone unlike Asherah, the goddess
of the groin, whom men worship with groans.
Men! They deify their desires! No, not
these gods. I have been seeking One who is
like … like nothing I have grasped but
many things I have glimpsed. As a girl,
I had a lamb that came when I called
its name. And I used to put flowers
in my hair—gathering them from the fields
that now, it seems, will never again be green.
Also, I remember how the rainbows
used to hurt my heart with their hints
of promises and purity. But not just
as a girl, though certainly it was keener,
cleaner, then. As a woman: our son
in my womb and later at my breast.
And the way my husband stroked my face
and smiled just before he died.
Yes, for all the grief, I've had glimpses.
This is the One I long for—the God
behind the glimpses. Someone good.
Someone who would make sense of life,
of living. Someone … Oh!
You know my meaning, or don't know, so
there's either no need or no way of telling.
One night I went to sleep, weeping,
and woke to the sound of a voice—
a soft, far voice like the stutter of a flame,
quiet, intermittent, quick—
that said, 'Soon. Soon.' I woke my son
and said, 'Soon, a deliverer.' But

it was a deception. In the morning,
it was hot. It has not rained
since. For a year, no rain. Our food
has dwindled. Soon, a slow death.
In the half-light of dawn this morning,
as I squatted by the ashes of the cooking fire,
a fly bothered me. When I waved it away,
the air unsettled the white ash,
which wafted and wobbled like goose-down
in the hearth. And as it shifted
I saw, briefly, for an instant only,
a small coal, bright as a rubbed ruby.
I claim no meanings. I simply say,
This morning I caught a glimpse of crimson,
a glimmer of warmth beneath the cold ashes.

Going to Zarephath
Elijah

I followed the brook-bed down
to the Jordan River, drinking on the way
from puddles of brackish water.
The river was sluggish and turning
to salt. I washed as I crossed.
On the plain, with each step,
the dust spurted from my sandals
like spore from a puff-ball fungus.
It was hot. The air shifted
and shimmered above the parched land.
A raven perched on a carcass,
glistened blue-black as sin
on the rib-cage of a bull,
tugging a scrap of hide from a bone.
It cocked its head and winked
as I passed. At the outskirts
of the first town I approached,

two children fled from me, screaming.
Their strength failed well short
of the first house and they flopped
down exhausted. They lay panting
like small birds that have flown
too far in the heat. I strode
to them, stood over them, my shadow
shielding them from the scorching sun.
Their eyes were big in their gaunt faces.
Stick limbs and bloated bellies.
I tried to speak but no words came.
I stooped to caress their cheeks
but they croaked in horror.
I left them huddled on the hard
hot earth and skirted around the town.
Barely one year and already
the children and the animals …
I journeyed on to the gentiles,
avoiding my own people on the way,
lest they should break my heart
and with it my resolve.

Gathering Sticks
The widow

I was gathering sticks by the city gate
when he came from the desert.
He looked dishevelled, dirty. He drew near
as if he knew me. Mad, I thought
and stepped back. Then he asked for water.
Water, of all things! But his voice defied
my definition. There was kindness there,
and courtesy. His accent announced
him as a Jew. There is a treaty
between our countries since our princess
slipped beneath a quilt to become

their queen. A compact but not compassion.
We have a history of hatred. Jeering
at Jews, some say, is one of life's joys.
And yet this man spoke with respect—
respect for me and for himself.
He neither begged nor bullied. He asked
for a drink in a way that made me
think I ought to thank him. The well
is within the walls. Quite a walk.
And yet I dropped my wood and went
willingly. Foreigners are forbidden water.
Unless, of course, they pay. Since
the drought, only citizens may draw it
free, though not freely. The rations
are stingy, the soldiers strict. But
I had yet to drop my bucket to fill my jar
for the day. It cost me nothing to save him
the money he did not have. I wanted
to do it. I felt a bond. We who are about
to die can at least be decent to each other.
Decency—it's one of the glimpses.
And so I dropped my sticks and turned back
to the gate. In the space of two steps
I remembered the voice—or did I hear it?—
'Soon. Soon.' And as my heart leapt
like a hart with thoughts of deliverance,
the man called out, 'And please,
make me also a cake to eat.' I staggered
with despair. My 'deliverer'? He brought nothing
but an empty belly for the last of my bread!

At the Sight of Her
Elijah

She was gathering sticks by the city gate
when I arrived. My heart sank at the sight

of her. She was herself in want, so
how could she help me? Had I heard amiss
God's voice? Nothing made sense.
'To Zarephath, which belongs to Sidon.'
Four days across the desert to a town
under the jurisdiction of Ethbaal, Jezebel's
father. To a woman, and a widow
at that. And then to find her gathering
sticks to cook the last of her food.
It was against all reason. Yet what
is poverty except an opportunity
for the providence of God? Is his strength
limited by our weakness? Is his hand short
that it cannot save? He fed a nation
by the miracle of manna. Are three people
too many for him? When I asked
the widow for food, she said, 'I have enough
for one meal for two—my son and me.'
Given the circumstance, there could be
no ignoring God's grace. By faith
I uttered an oracle. 'Fear not. The flour
and oil shall not fail, until the day
the Lord sends rain upon the earth.' Until,
by my word, the day of drenching.
Might not God multiply the oil without
the olive berry? Must he work only
through sap and seasons? May not he
bypass the tree? And the meal—must it
always come first from the ear and the mill?
'Fear not,' I said. Did she believe?
Perhaps. Or mayhap she thought it no longer
mattered. Whatever, she did as I bade—
brought water, baked a cake and gave it
to me. Steam rose like incense from its crust.
It tasted fine. It tasted like
the bread the ravens brought, only hot, hot.

One Meal More
The widow

I was wrong. There was enough
for three. I mixed the oil with the meal
and baked the dough on the coals.
I broke a piece for the prophet,
the remainder for my son and myself.
We ate in silence. He dabbed the crumbs
from his plate then asked for a place
to sleep. I prepared him a bed
in the room on the roof of the house.
When he'd settled I looked in the jar.
No oil, bar a film on the fired clay.
The barrel, too, was empty—merely
a dusting of flour on the floor. So, a liar
was lying in my bed, having eaten the last
of my bread. Shame on the shaman!
Shame on the fool who fell for his sham!
The oil spent, the flour failed, despite
every word he'd said. And yet at dusk
when he woke he asked for more.
More bread for his blasphemous mouth!
I lifted the lid to the jar. 'You said—'
I scoffed, then stopped. In the pot
was a cupful of oil, glistening like honey
in the gloaming. And the flour—
three scoops in a heap in the barrel!
Though it ought to have been relief,
bitterness replaced my disbelief. True,
it was a miracle, but a mingy one
at best. In the face of months of famine,
the prophet's God, the mighty God
of Israel, gave from his bountiful store
barely enough for one meal more!

from
The Colour of Life
2011

The Colour of Life

Why is it that here in this café—
a hard wind harmless on the window,
a bright fire coughing in the grate,
scones and tea on the table—I feel

suddenly, strangely sad? Why is it,
and what? A loneliness, a longing—
not, it seems, in spite of, but
because of, the loveliest of things.

It is the colour of life. *Sabi*,
the haiku poets would say. I say
too much. I break a scone and steam
wafts from the wound, like

the spirit of a just man, going home.

Delay

If I get going,
as I should, when again will
I hear things as sweet
as these swallow-twitterings
from the wires in the street?

The Gravity of the Slight

Gravity can grab
even something as slight as
a dragonfly wing.
Look, the ends of the still blades
are dipping towards the earth.

Finishing Up

Nightfall ... and I am still here
in the school at the prison farm.

My children will be at the table, filling
their mouths with food and chatter.

And the littlest one will be asking
her mother, 'Where is Daddy?'

I am where my resignation
has led me. My roguish students

are in the compound, locked up
for the night. Except for the sentries

the guards are gone. I am alone,
finishing up. Did I miss someone

when I said goodbye? Does it matter?
We have been good to one another,

these bad men and I. I try not
to think I will never see them again.

I am alone. I look out the window.
The forest is in silhouette.

On the lawn, almost dissolved
in the dusk, a young kangaroo

hunches on its haunches to graze.
It was not there a moment ago and

in a moment when I open the door
it will not be there again.

Prayer Against Pain

If you love me still
oh Lord make me well

Let your goodness spill
to this place I fell

Lift me by your will
high above this hell

By your power kill
pain's clangour and knell

Let my body fill
with harm's last farewell

And my being thrill
with cruelty's quell

Oh Lord make me still
if you love me well

Bird and Bull

The dotterel,
stalking, sniping—so little
by the muzzle
and muddy hoof of the bull
drinking at the dam's puddle.

Signal

As I lift the mug,
light reflects from its glazing
in the black window—
faint and intermittent like
a lighthouse signal, far off.

Human

Not ingratitude
but ... human ... to be feeling
on the quiet beach
towards sunset in autumn
such loneliness and longing.

Me

'In this mortal frame
of mine ... there is something ...'
Yes, it's me ... and I
feel this *me* always yearning
for something that is not me.

Haijin and Violet

I
Suggestion

i

A haijin suggests
to a little mauve violet—
try this one for size.

ii

Oh Master Bashō,
did you know you'd formed a form
just right for violets?

iii

Rescued by haiku—
a little violet smothered
in its own foliage.

II
Reflection

i

The master's violets
held in haiku and haiga—
still strangely touching.

ii

Across the centuries
the same sweet flowers—Bashō's
haiga of violets.

iii

About these violets—
conveying to the knowing
a breath of Bashō.

III
Realisation

i

A haiku moment—
suddenly realising God
has violets in mind.

ii

These divine violets—
who'd have thought the Almighty
imagined such things?

iii

These violet violets—
more outstanding haiku from
the Divine Haijin.

Heat
19 January 1991, third day of the Gulf War, Desert Storm

I wake exhausted from the heat.
Dreams will not drift to me again
today. Resentfully, I rise, dress
and leave the house. The street

is empty, evacuated by sleep.
It's barely six but already the sun
is rising above the rooftops
like a rocket with kills to keep.

From one house, news of the war
—that earnest, incessant drone
of the announcer's voice!—sorties
from a radio through an open door.

Perhaps the Great Assize
swirls in the dusts of the Desert
Storm. Halfway round the world
warplanes are rising to the skies.

Worship

Released from
Sunday School
the children

are chasing
grasshoppers
on the lawn.

Jumbled and
jolly, they
creep and jump.

Leaping up,
my soul is
snatched mid-air.

After Death

Even those
who doubt
Christ's claim
that

after death
comes judgment

even those
are troubled
by certainty
that

after death
comes forever …

Prayer

Oh, for my mother in her pain,
Almighty and all-loving Lord,
I come to plead with you again.

For years her body's been a bane
That's put all gladness to the sword:
Oh, for my mother in her pain!

Too much misery makes a stain
To black all light and block all laud:
I come to plead with you again.

Today at least relieve the strain
And give reprieve as a reward,
Oh, for my mother in her pain.

I know there is no other Name.
Despite the fact my faith is flawed,
I come to plead with you again.

Although my many sins maintain
That I deserve to be ignored—
Oh, for my mother in her pain
I come to plead with you again!

End of Day

We pass the cows on their way
   to the milking shed
and the farmer's easing hands.

Frogs are gladly chorusing
   like little gibbons
in the dark reeds by the soak.

We cross the fallow paddock
   to a stand of trees
surrounded by burnt bracken.

The fire has found a refuge
   in the deep hollow
at the base of a dead tree.

In the absence of rabbits
   I slip back the bolt
and lay the rifle aside.

My sons collect sticks and roots
   to stoke the jarrah
tree's self-consuming furnace.

A pair of pygmy bats hunt
   and even dogfight
in the twilight and the smoke.

'Did you bring the bullet, Dad?'
   I toss the cartridge
that misfired into the fire.

We run for cover and cheer
   in shock and joy at
the expected explosion.

We are happy together
   my small sons and I
here at the dark end of day.

from
Inadvertent Things:
Poems in traditional Japanese forms
2013

Envy

I watch with envy
the small birds in the bamboo.
So *now* and happy!
They at least need not review
what they did or did not do.

Going Down

As on a treadmill,
a woman on the steps of
the escalator—
beckoning a small boy who
fears to join her going down.

Meditations on Pain

      i

Distilling my life
to *now, now* and *this, this*—
the pain I'm feeling.

      ii

A fish in its pond
is hardly more immersed than
my life in its pain.

      iii

Innumerable—
the minutes in an hour since
pain began counting.

      iv

This persistent pain—
drawing all thoughts into one
cloud of unknowing.

Azure

Surely a piece is
missing from the azure robe
of the Madonna
in some ancient mosaic
because of that fairy wren!

Tweezers

As with tweezers
a woman pincers precisely
an eyebrow hair—
a honeyeater plucks aphids
from the calyx of a white rose.

Waterlily Haiku

    i

In a red gown—
the carp beneath the lily's
green parasol.

    ii

A disturbance ...
and then those undulations
in the lily-pads.

    iii

Whenever I look
there's never a frog folded
on the lily-pads.

    iv

The missing goldfish—
wafting out from the shadows
of the lily leaves.

    v

The waterlily—
floating another helipad
for the dragonflies.

Daffodils

      i

First daffodils—
she worries they will be hurt
by the hard rain.

      ii

The daffodils—
my wife goes after the rain
to pick me some.

      iii

Three daffodils—
reluctantly, she leaves one
in the garden.

Binoculars

My sons, like possums,
climbing in the loquat tree ...
I pause to watch them
through the small binoculars
they gave me for Father's Day.

Radiance

I recall it still,
that look on her face after
the long agony—
that radiance as she held
our baby red with her blood.

Beloved

      i

Disturbing the lines
of her torso and my thought—
the curve of her breast.

      ii

Shower recess
beaded with water ricocheted
from her body.

      iii

She suckles the baby
then comes to me … her body's
loved by everybody!

Kangaroo Haiku

    i

Out in the scrub
rising up then sinking down
kangaroo heads.

    ii

First rain … an odour
of kangaroos in the hollow
between the grasstrees.

    iii

Slightly more solid
than the twilight—kangaroos
crossing the firebreak.

    iv

The kangaroos—
gathering in the paddock
with the darkness.

Wren Haiku

      i

Resting in a ring
in the rusted wire-netting—
a blue fairy wren.

      ii

Thin as wire, the legs
of the fairy wren perching
in the chicken wire.

      iii

Surprise cameo—
a circle of wire holding
an opaline wren.

      iv

Wishing I could send
my wife that wren in the wire
as a love locket.

Stargazing

The binoculars,
as if I had Parkinson's,
refuse to steady.
So the stars zigzag about
like crazy, brilliant midges.

Navigation

Though navigators
can find their way by the stars,
I look and am lost.
The only place they lead me,
my Sovereign, is home to you.

Squid Haiku

    i

Squinting at an ink
blot on the pier … what's it mean,
this squid Rorschach test?

    ii

Luminous, the green
mascara the captured squid
has put on for death.

    iii

In shock from the hook
that turned it into live bait,
the squid gently sinks …

    iv

Ink blot on the pier—
read no more into it than
the death of a squid.

Black Dog, Snarling

When it bared its teeth
at me again, the black dog,
I bared, bared my neck.
But it would no more attack
than it would go, go on back!

Black Dog, Dozing

Waking, I am not
surprised to sense the black dog
dozing at my feet.
Today I must try harder
not to toss it scraps of meat.

Creators

And after bamboos
in all uprightness the Lord
made human beings …
And seeing bamboos growing
these image-bearers
at once imagined wind-chimes
xylophones and flutes …
And later as things fell out
arrows, blowpipes and war-fans.

Seeing the Sound

As to the eye
the springing of the mallets
so to the ear
the bounding of the poundings
from the taut timpani skins.

Purity

The notes are flat
and the timing is out, yet
what pure music
they make, the little sawn lengths
of bamboo bumped by breezes.

Small Matters

    i

Atoms, genes, haiku—
foolish to dismiss them as
merely small matters.

    ii

The haiku poets
appreciate small matters
affect heart matters.

    iii

Like science, haiku
demonstrate that nothing is
too small to matter.

    iv

Like Jesus, haiku
perceive the tree in the seed
and birds in the tree.

    v

Being small matters
haiku provide a way of
seeing small matters.

    vi

To see small matters
and to see that *small* matters
are not small matters.

Pause

Does he ever pause,
the shearer, to take pleasure
in the way his comb,
stroke by stroke, colours the sheep
such a clean and creamy white?

Sheep

Only three days since
they were shorn and already
their whiteness is gone.
Still, who of us has managed
even that long in this world?

Samurai

Like the samurai
I long not to shame myself
or my Lord in death.
Yet those ancient warriors
are beyond compare
in bare courage and resolve.
I fear I'll never
match such mighty ones as them.
Yet my Lord avers:
Not your courage but my grace
will defend you from disgrace.

Black Bamboo

    i

Empathy today
with the ebony bamboo—
this empty feeling.

    ii

This feeling—something
that's escaped from the centre
of a bamboo cane.

    iii

Hollow … I suppose
the bamboo by my window
always feels this way.

    iv

Again I wake
with a hollow feeling—oh,
my bamboo heart!

    v

Hollow, like the black
bamboo … if only I had
its composure, too.

    vi

Lord, may not music
come from emptiness? Oh make
a flute of my heart!

Reflection

I stop to ask if
he's hurt, the young man lying
on the damp grass at
midnight. He says he's thinking
about how his life's gone wrong.

Seize the Day

It's all right for *them,*
the waking birds who in grace
chirp, *Carpe diem!*
They've no reckoning to face
here or any other place.

from
*Distillations
of Different Lands*
2018

Forgetting

'I long to pick/ Some forgetting-grass' —
Ki no Tsurayuki, The Tosa Diary, 935 AD

For you I need a different flower,
brother, than the blue forget-me-nots.

Here, here in this world where you left me
I yearn for the sweet forgetting-grass

treasured by the ancient Japanese.
I want to search out and gather up

those grasses that take away grieving
by somehow infusing forgetting.

I want stooks of the stuff, large wigwam
stooks that can be shaken loose and strewn

to cover me with stalk, leaf and scent
from the loss of you and how you went.

Recollections of Dread and Deliverance

Dearest, when you haemorrhaged
(I am of a sudden with hurt and horror
recalling it these near-three decades on),

when back in the ward after the birthing
the nurse drew down from your white face
the bedcover to uncover that swamp

of blood from your wounded womb,
that crimson saturation of nightdress
and sheet, I plunged to pleas and please!

And when they wheeled you on the trolley
away to the theatre, not now for new life
but for your life, I feared you'd gone for good

but by the doctor's good hand the hand
of God touched you, staunched you, spared you
for me and our newborn daughter and all

the other loved ones who loved you
as I loved you and love you still with kisses
and wide wishes and everlasting longings.

Afterphase
for Susan

In the loll and lull
of love's afterphase

her face is flushed,
her hair is mussed and

her mouth is curved
in shy contentment,

signalling her heart
shares her body's

softness towards me.

Dove Tanka Triptych

1
Landing

A backbeating dove
landing alongside its mate
on the birdbath rim
has one slender slat missing
from the grey fan of its tail.

2
Stepping

Like a lumberjack
negotiating floating logs
cautiously a dove
stepping with little slippings
across the new-cut bamboo.

3
Drinking

A sudden flurry
and the dove on the birdbath
is gone, gone into
the paws and jaws of next-door's
low-hiding high-leaping cat.

Wire Wrens

      i

Beside a white hen,
in the wire of the chook run,
a female blue wren.

      ii

Passing through yet
the wren pauses a moment
in the wire net.

      iii

Just a set of hoops
for the wrens—the wire netting
of the chicken coop.

Prank Call

In my dream I breathed heavily
into the telephone mouthpiece.

I was wanting to make a sound,
send a sensation, of menace

down the pathways of wire and air
to set the caller's heart quailing.

I breathed heavily in my dream,
lacing each lung-gust with a growl,

until I was stopped, mortified,
by a voice wheezy with asthma

and love, a voice saying my name.
And as I dreamed I woke I said,

'Oh Mother, Mother, forgive me!'
But she never did, being dead.

Dearly Departed

So much of it, my childhood,
departed this world with you.

Though I lived it, I can bring back
only brief moments of it:

candle-smoke and a blue trike,
a Band-Aid on a skinned knee,

your bosomy hugs during
nights of dread dreams about ... what?

Mother, I meant to ask you
so many things about me,

so many whens, hows and whys
that can never now be known.

The loss of both your presence
and my history presses on me

as an ever-present absence.

Koi Pond Tanka

    1

It is the late
and lingering light that koi find
most marvellous:
I watch them moseying about
under their roof of reflections.

    2

Silvery and svelte,
a sodden bamboo leaf lifts
and lilts like a koi
from the bottom of the pond
on the current of the hose.

    3

Near nightfall, the koi
rise up and touch their foreheads
to their reflections
the way Maori touch noses
when fondly greeting their friends.

Reading at Lunchtime

A drop I squeezed
from a lemon slice

missed the plate
of battered fish

and hit the book
of Chinese poems—

fell, to my distress,
on a stanza by

an unknown poet
Confucius included

in *The Book of Songs*
he compiled

500 years before
the first coming of

the Man of Sorrows.
Such a bitter drop—

on the clean paper
it left a stain like a tear.

T'ao Ch'ien and the End of Things

T'ao Ch'ien, that gentle long-ago
Chinese poet of fields and gardens,
opined that, when it ends, life
returns into an empty absence.

This is, to be sure, the good stuff
of pining poetry, this thought
of the waiting absence, the calling
emptiness. How it moves us!

Such heroism, to press ahead despite
the hopelessness! Such nobility,
to be wilfully looking to the stars
while knowingly bound for the abyss!

But do we really return to an empty
absence? Surely it is an absence
to which we return only if
it is an absence from which we come?

Lao Tze was, I guess, the sage
by whom Ch'ien was enlightened
to believe the Tao is the Way
from emptiness to emptiness. But

I too revere the ancient teachings
about beginnings and endings.
I too yield to the wisdom of the sages
in matters of spirit and eternity.

And I weigh the Tao Te Ching
against the Ecclesiastes. The writer
of this sacred text pondered
meanings and purposes, and out-

matched even the Eastern masters
in mourning for our mortality.
Yet he concluded that when life's
pitcher is shattered at the fountain

the spirit returns to God who gave it
and he will either judge or save it.

Travelling North

The Canada geese go over,
fly over in a skein,
high up and (I imagine)
honking beyond hearing.

And I suddenly wonder,
What am I doing here
in America travelling north
deeper into Wisconsin

where the first snows
have already fallen,
travelling north when
even the geese know

the killing cold is coming
and south is the place to go?

Canada Geese Near Canada

1

A spearhead of geese,
fixed on the shaft of instinct,
and hurled by autumn—
how swiftly and straight it flies
south in the threatening skies!

2

Again, skeins of geese
cross the Wisconsin border,
wearing the sky's fleece.
And whose heart doesn't shiver
for want of a warmer winter?

3

If not for one thing
I'd follow those geese across
the United States …
their farthest south is far north
of where my beloved waits.

4

The Canada geese
have begun their migration.
Will it ever cease?
I gaze at their formation
with ache and resignation.

The Martyred Mother
i.m. Hashimoto Tecla and her children, Kyoto, 1619 AD

I speak not of the other four children
who were condemned with her, nor even of
the newest child in her womb, but only
of the smallest one bound to her bosom.

One might have imagined the rope would burn
through fast so the baby's body would fall
away from hers—slump free from the torso
to which it was tied as if to a stake.

And yet it seems the persecutors' cord
bore the flames better than the martyrs' flesh.
Perhaps they had soaked that rope in water
before they wrapped it around their victims.

Still, hemp's surely coarser, tougher than flesh.
How long would it take for flames to fray it?
Longer, I guess, than it would take to melt
fat in an infant's cheek, a woman's breast.

Whether wet or dry, thick or thin, that rope
held out long enough for the flames to fuse
the child to its mother's chest, meld the two
into one greasy charred misshapen lump.

On the fumie the faithful won't trample
the carved Madonna clasps the destined Child—
in like manner, but with bound and burned arms,
the martyred mother held her infant fast.

And in this embrace both she and the babe
defied the shogun and exposed his shame.
Their souls rode up in palanquins of smoke,
up to their Sovereign, who wept as they came.

The Crimson Maples
i.m. the Kakure Kirishitan

It is their glory,
the Japanese autumn maples,
to look so gory …
enacting the martyrs' burning,
depicting the Saviour's blooding.

New & Uncollected Poems

Visiting Bashō's Grave
Gichuji Temple, Otsu, Japan

     i

Modest, like haiku—
Master Matsuo Bashō's
memorial stone.

     ii

With pulley and pale,
though both a little weathered—
Bashō's temple well.

     iii

Bashō would like it—
the imperfect re-joining
of his split headstone.

     iv

Bashō and wabi—
the wood of the hooped bucket
discoloured by rust.

     v

Bashō or Issa?
A turtle piggybacking
a smaller turtle.

     vi

A little apart
from Bashō's gravestone and hut—
look, banana trees!

Didgeridoo Player
Minoh Quasi-National Park, Osaka Prefecture, Japan

    1
Dreaming

Am I dreaming
or is … is it The Dreaming
I hear droning?
Listen, by a stream in Japan,
a didgeridoo-playing man!

    2
Mesmerising

A low mutter
smoothly intermingling with
a light murmur …
mesmerising, this duet
of didgeridoo and stream.

    3
Yearning

It sets me yearning,
the surprising deep droning
from a man blowing
a piece of plastic piping
to sounds of water running.

Incidentals
Kyoto Spring

      i

Level water
betraying the stone basin's
lopsidedness.

      ii

Was it a wind-gust
or a sparrow-arrival—
the petal-scatter?

      iii

A cut bamboo
creating in the mosses
a small crater.

      iv

Trickling water
stopped by a little levee
of cherry petals.

      v

Incidentals—
buoyant on the bowl water,
fallen petals.

Dip

A little dip
in the broad rim

directs the brim-
ming rainwater

where to over-
flow, gliding slow

or quick in drib-
ble, drip or drop,

from the wide cup
of the level-

standing garden
granite basin.

Bamboo Forest, Arashiyama

    i

Incessant waves—
the kamikaze sweeping
the bamboos' staves.

    ii

Sounding alarms—
in the bamboo forest those
clashing polearms.

    iii

With sky for dojo—
the giant timber bamboos
practising kendo.

On the Substitution Monkey Charms of Kyoto and Nara
Ball-like red cloth Migawari-zaru *(substitution monkey) charms are believed to 'protect sinners from punishment by Kōshin, as the monkey (Kōshin's messenger) is punished instead.'*

1

Punish the monkey
is the appeal of this charm
offered to the god:
for my bad, give it the blame;
for my hurt, give it the harm.

2

Beliefs a monkey
can stand for a man seem cute.
But compared to us
the ancients were quite astute,
knowing we need a substitute.

3

The principle,
I suggest, is sound, but not
the principal:
I doubt it's a monkey who's
suited to stand in our shoes.

4

Substitutes must be
equal to or greater than …
So if a monkey
can't take the place of a man
is there Anyone else who can?

Temple Ladle
Hozen Temple, Osaka, Japan

This bamboo ladle
laying across the worn rim
of a stone basin
brimming with water poured from
a plastic bucket
filled from a hand-pump plumbing
a plank-covered well
where a white cat is lounging—
this bamboo ladle
waits for the next devotee
to grip and dip it
then swing it up to scatter
cool water onto
the moss-covered figure of
a Buddhist guardian god.

The Bodhisattva's Bib
Jizō, guardian of the souls of miscarried and aborted children

    i

Instead of her child,
she ties the cloth bib around
the worn Jizō stone.

    ii

Flat now, her tummy—
like the weathered stone Jizō
she's dressing in red.

    iii

Never to know yuck—
the bib she has tied around
the stone Jizō's neck.

    iv

Unlike the colour
of the bib the sun will leach—
her unfading grief.

The Mother, the Bosatsu, and the Water Child

    1
Pebble

'For my mizuko,'
a mother says to Jizō,
setting a pebble
at his stone feet in the hope
he will pass it on to help.

    2
Bonnet and Bib

Seeing them still there
on Jizō, the bonnet and bib,
the sad mother asks,
'Why haven't you taken them
to clothe my child in limbo?'

    3
Atonement

Seemingly, the child
deserves to be punished in
Buddhist purgatory
for the distress her death caused
the mother who aborted her.

4
Mizuko Kuyō

She comes to Jizō,
the mother grieving her child …
In care and mercy,
he is the Buddhist Jesus …
And yet, and yet, is he real?

5
Saviour

If only her hope,
the sorrowful mother, were
not in stone Jizō
but in sweet Jesus, lover
of all the darling lost souls!

Jizō Stones by the Three-Storied Pagoda
Kōfuku-ji, Nara

Treading softly the deer
graze among the Jizō stones

where mothers shed a tear
for their aborted children

and try to stem their fear
that the children suffer there

the hell they suffered here.

Idol Stones

The hour is coming
when idols will be worshipped
no more: every heart
will soften and the mountains
will reclaim their stolen stones.

First Blood

Hours before the souls
of the first sinners were washed
with the sacred blood,
the roots of the olive trees
were bathed in Gethsemane.

Apprehension

As we amble in autumn in Nara Park,
where cherries and ginkgoes are turning stark

and stags scent the heat of hinds on the breeze,
my soul apprehends as my sight perceives

the heart-shaped leaves of the Chinese tallows,
crimson as blood from the Man of Sorrows.

Windbells at Fushimi Inari Shrine

     1
Beckoning

A shop at the shrine
selling big-tailed stone foxes
and toy-sized torii
has a dangle of windbells,
all dinging with the wind's dint.

     2
Resonance

The resonance of
this petite, perfectly-pitched
caste-iron windbell
lingers as frail and fair as
the sea-sound in a seashell.

     3
Sacredness

There is everything
and nothing sacred about
this Shinto windbell
whose fashioned material
sounds out the ethereal.

4
Charmed

I will take it home
and hang it in the bamboos
by my writing room,
this small Japanese windbell
that has charmed me with its chime.

Autumn Maples, Kyoto

      i

Kyoto autumn—
the colder the air, the warmer
the maple leaves.

      ii

Doubly lovely—
the maples turning beside
the temple pond.

      iii

Teahouse umbrella—
a little faded under
the autumn maples.

      iv

Temple fire buckets—
optimistic considering
the autumn maples.

The Easter Trees

1
The Succour Trees

In Gethsemane
olives were the only ones
(excluding angels)
who stood by the Son of God
as he wept and sweated blood.

2
The Empathy Trees

What causes maples
round Eastertime to redden?
It was not *their* roots
that were rinsed in the garden
by drops of the Saviour's blood.

3
The Carpenter Tree

It's a wonder life
didn't sprout from the sawn wood,
leafy sprigs of it,
where the nails were hammered in,
driving his blood through the grain.

Gleam

The water pooled
in the stone bowl

has on its skin
a scarlet gleam

from a nearby
paper lantern

and in its depths
several goldfish

upon whose scales
the gleam gathers.

Bamboo Dragonflies

1
Balance

Bamboo dragonflies
float above scribbles and drafts
on my writing desk.
Just the sight of them can impart
balance to my unbalanced heart.

2
Reflection

They waft as I write,
like hawks hovering, two deft
bamboo dragonflies:
I, too, could pose with such poise
if spared life's billows and blows.

3
Diversion

For diversion
I puff and cuff to make them
dip and dither—
the bamboo dragonflies on
my desk from distant Japan.

Little Endings

     i

The spider's mistake—
as it approached it set me
doing the quick-step!

     ii

Worse for the snail—
hearing while night-walking that
unexpected crunch!

     iii

My condolences,
grasshopper, for hopping into
the child's affections.

     iv

Howzat! The blowfly
scored a triple twenty on
the spider's dartboard!

     v

A grim irony—
aiming at a spider with
a can of fly-spray.

     vi

Feeling a bit flat—
mosquito meditating
on a clapping sound.

Bamboo Triptych

1
Weather-Wasted

How light the sun-split
pieces of bamboo have become
since first they were cut:
whoever would have supposed
that sap could be so heavy?

2
Aerosol Airs

Spraying ants nesting
inside the sawn bamboo tubes,
I'm surprised by sighs
mellow and mournful as notes
from Zen shakuhachi flutes.

3
Little Logs

Splitting with dryness,
these bamboo pieces I've sawn.
Yet, scattered or piled,
they're so imbued with beauty
I can hardly bear to burn them.

In the Gardens of the Imperial Palace
for Susan, Kyoto

      i

She takes a turn
in the gardens ... the maples
redden and burn.

      ii

Her greatest fans—
the ginkgoes offer my love
their golden fans.

      iii

The sparrows whir—
even they are unsettled
at the sight of her.

Faces

Even the faces
of a cherry tree aren't as
delicately flushed
as my beloved's face since
we lay together in love.

This Woman

And after Jesus
I'll ask the Father's consent
to speak of Susan.
And I'll say, 'I, too, want to
bear witness to this woman.'

This Tinnitus

       i

This tinnitus—
its tintinnabulations
so whiningly thin!

       ii

This tinnitus—
tiny and tinny and yet
so terribly loud!

       iii

This tinnitus—
its flatline shrilling is so
utterly tireless!

       iv

This tinnitus—
unresolvable until
the resurrection.

Radiance
after the Apostle, 2 Corinthians 4:6

Writing the night away
I watch the whitening
of the dawn sky.

And I see the sun
rise up in its radiance
like its Maker,

the oneandonly God
who said, 'Let light shine
out of darkness',

and it did—truly it
shone in my heart
to give me the light

of the knowledge
of his great glory
in the face of Christ!

Endnotes

Crabbing
The large swimmer crabs (*Portunus armatus*) caught in the beach waters and estuaries of south-western Australia are known locally as 'blue manna crabs'.

A Remembrance of Robins
Australian scarlet robins (*Petroica boodang*) are small, shy birds, perhaps a third the size of an American robin. Because of the patch of white on their foreheads, they are sometimes called white-capped robins.

Dugite
Dugites (*Pseudonaja affinis*) are highly venomous snakes native to south-western Australia.

On Haiku
The haiku is a distinctive poetic form conceived and refined in 17th century Japan. Structurally, haiku consist of 17 syllables arranged in 3 lines of 5, 7, 5 syllables each. Plainly, brevity is a defining feature of haiku, and this brevity is achieved and animated through the use of such literary techniques as precision, concision, juxtaposition, allusion and ellipsis.

Although some consider the traditional 5-7-5-syllabic pattern to be unnecessary for English-language haiku, it is nonetheless the pattern that I have chosen to work within. Even those haiku in *Abundance* that deviate from this structural ideal owe their incarnation in large measure to it.

'On Haiku' summarises my understanding of how haiku work and expresses my aim in writing them.

With the exception of two ('Ford' and 'On Haiku'), the haiku in *Abundance* are arranged in suites, or sets, known as gunsaku. A gunsaku is not a single poem written in haiku stanzas, nor is it a series of haiku that are arranged in sequence and depend upon or develop from one another. (Such a progression of interlocking haiku is known as a rensaku.) Rather, it is a gathering, an assembly, of independent haiku that share a common subject, setting, theme or mood. Each haiku in a gunsaku is a complete and self-contained poem (my use of numbering is intended to help the reader appreciate this), and yet the meaning and emotion of each one is enriched by its association with the others, and together they form a kind of compound poem, making something bigger than themselves without losing themselves. At least, this is my theory and my hope!

The Weight of the Baby
Marron (*Cherax cainii*) are freshwater crayfish native to the south-west of Western Australia. They grow to triple the size of Louisiana crawfish.

Mopokes are a species of owl—Southern Boobook Owl (*Ninox novaeseelandiae*). Found throughout Australia, their colloquial name mimics their night calls.

Shock
I was at the time working on the second novel (*Dragonfox*) in my fantasy trilogy, *The Chronicles of Klarin*. Hence, quite literally 'I was writing about dragons …'

Journey
Matsuo Bashō (1644-1694), arguably the greatest of all Japanese haiku poets, wrote *The Narrow Road to the Deep North* (*Oku no Hosomich*) about a walking journey he undertook in northern Japan in 1689. His acclaimed travel journal is in the form of a haibun, a literary work consisting of sparse prose interspersed with haiku.

For additional notes on Basho, see under 'Visiting Bashō's Grave'.

Gladdened by Ibises
Kikuyu is an introduced grass (from Africa) that used to be grown as lawns in suburban homes and parks in Western Australia and is still grown for fodder in some dairy farms. If not mown or cropped, it can grow knee-high.

Brimming
Wagtails—more commonly called willie wagtails (*Rhipidura leucophrys*)—are common birds in Australia and are a species of fantail. As their name suggests, they are restive birds, constantly swinging and fanning their tails and often chatter harshly, as if scolding.

The Worship Tanka
There are 80 tanka in *Abundance*, many of them arranged in sets (see notes on gunsaku under 'On Haiku'). Like the haiku, the tanka (or waka) is a traditional Japanese poetic form, although it predates the haiku by 1,000 years.

Also like the haiku, the tanka is structured in 5- and 7-syllable lines. It consists of 31 syllables arranged in 5 lines of 5, 7, 5, 7, 7 syllables each. I have worked towards this syllabic ideal in the tanka in *Abundance*.

Again, as with the haiku, there are numerous subtleties and possibilities associated with the tanka form. It is wonderfully adaptable, and can be lyrical, imagist or descriptive in style and can accommodate almost any subject, theme and mood.

Although I became interested in tanka early in my writing life, and although they are represented in all my poetry collections, it was not until recent years that I quite fell in love with the form. Indeed, two of my last three poetry collections—*Kyoto Momiji Tanka: poems and photographs of Japan in autumn* and *Kyoto Sakura Tanka* (neither of which, for reasons of space, are represented in this selected works)—consist solely of poems written in the tanka form. I find the brevity of the form helps me to refine and concentrate my thoughts, which in turn helps me to distil the essence of a subject, situation or scene, while working towards the syllabic line measures helps me to shape the phrasing and unfolding of the poem.

Me
Quotation from Matsuo Bashō, 'Learn from the Pine'.

Haijin and Violet
A haijin is a person who writes haiku, a haiku poet.

Traditionally, a haiku poet might sometimes include an inkbrush painting on the same sheet of paper on which a haiku is written. Such austere, Japanese-style paintings are known at haiga, 'haiku drawings'. More than an illustration, the painting is a visual distillation of the haiku it accompanies.

For 'haiku', see notes under 'On Haiku'.

The Martyred Mother
Fumie were small plaques with images of Jesus or Mary and were used to identify Christians during the Tokugawa shogunate: people who refused to tread on them revealed themselves as Christians and were tortured and (unless they apostatised) gruesomely executed.

Visiting Bashō's Grave
Matsuo Bashō (1644-1694) is the most famous of the traditional haiku poets of Japan. He stands first among the four great haiku masters—Yosa Buson (1716-1784), Kobayashi Issa (1763-1828) and Masaoka Shiki (1868-1902).

For addition notes on Basho, see under 'Journey'.

The Bodhisattva's Bib
For Japanese women worshippers, idols of Jizō represent not only the bodhisattva himself but also the children they have lost. By clothing Jizō stones and statues in bibs and bonnets, they both venerate Jizō and vicariously dress their naked, purgatory-bound children.

For 'bodhisattva' and 'Jizō' see notes under 'The Mother, the Bosatsu, and the Water Child'.

The Mother, the Bosatsu, and the Water Child
'Bosatsu' is the Japanese term for the Sanskrit term 'bodhisattva'.

In Buddhist belief, a bodhisattva is a being who has attained enlightenment but chooses not to adopt Buddhahood and enter nirvana in order to help other sentient beings attain enlightenment.

Jizō is a Buddhist bodhisattva (bosatsu) who is especially revered by women in Japan as the guardian of the souls of miscarried and aborted children.

The grief Japanese women feel for children they have miscarried or aborted is magnified by their belief that the souls of these children have gone to a Buddhist limbo, or purgatory, on the banks of a river called Sai no Kawara, where, naked and alone, they are compelled endlessly to pile stones for penance while being harried by demons.

Believing that Jizō Bosatsu is able to deliver their children from this torment, women adorn idols of Jizō (some as relief-carved stone slabs and others as stone or concrete sculptures in the round) with red bonnets and bibs, and offer them gifts of pebbles, toys and drinks.

'Mizuko' is a Japanese word meaning, literally, 'water child', and refers to a child who has died before birth.

'Mizuko kuyō'—literally, 'water child memorial service'—is a Japanese Buddhist ceremony centred on the worship of Jizō. Its purpose is to comfort women who have lost children by enabling them to express their regrets (via Jizō) to their lost children and to entreat Jizō to rescue them from the torments of Sai no Kawara.

Jizō Stones by the Three-Storied Pagoda
I have used the term 'Jizō stones' to describe the older stone 'sculptures' of Jizō. These narrow, slab-like stones are generally shaped like a blunted

spearhead, are less than 18 inches (45 cm) tall, 10 inches (25 cm) wide, and 4 inches (10 cm) thick at their thickest points in the middle and at the base. They are roughly relief-carved, so the featureless head and torso of Jizō bulges from the flat background of the stone. Some of them seem never to have been relief-carved at all, while many others are so weathered that the figure of Jizō is more imagined than seen. Sometimes these stones stand in groups on hillsides or in the precincts of Buddhist temples. Other times they stand alone or in pairs by roadsides and riversides. They are almost always clothed in bibs (which look more like aprons on the smaller stones), and often in bonnets, too.

For 'Jizō' see notes under 'The Mother, the Bosatsu, and the Water Child'.

The Easter Trees – 2. The Empathy Trees
In the southern hemisphere, and therefore Australia, Easter comes in autumn.

Acknowledgements

THE 'SELECTED' POEMS IN this collection are republished from the following eleven poetry collections: *Counterpoise* (Angus & Robertson Publishers, 1980); *Windfalls* (Fremantle Arts Centre Press, 1984); *Waking and Always* (Angus & Robertson Publishers, 1987); *The Grasshopper Heart* (William Collins/ Angus & Robertson Publishers, 1991); *Between Glances* (William Heinemann Australia, 1993); *Fontanelle* (Five Islands Press, 2004); *Birds in Mind: Australian nature poems* (Wombat Books, 2009); *From Far from Home: Poems of faith, grief and gladness* (Wombat Books, 2010); *The Colour of Life* (in *Two Poets* – Fremantle Press, 2011); *Inadvertent Things: Poems in traditional Japanese forms* (Walleah Press, 2013); and *Distillations of Different Lands* (Sunline Press, 2018).

Many poems in this collection were first published in the following magazines and newspapers:

The Age; *The Alternative*; *Amity*; *The Asahi Shimbun*; *Australian Poetry Journal*; *Antipodes*; *Artlook*; *The Briefing*; *The Bulletin*; *CAFHS Forum*; *Challenge*; *The Canberra Times*; *Captivated*; *Christians Writing*; *Chronicles*; *Eternity*; *Family Matters*; *First Things*; *Free eXpression*; *Hemisphere*; *The Horatian*; *Interaction*; *Life Insight*; *Life News*; *Linq*; *The Mainichi*; *Marginata*; *McMaster Journal of Theology & Ministry*; *Meanjin*; *Micropress New Zealand*; *Micropress Yates*; *The Mozzie*; *New Life*; *Nimrod*; *On Being*; *Overland*; *Patterns*; *Poetry Australia*; *Poetry Ireland Review*; *Quadrant*; *Rajasthan University Studies in English*; *Southerly*; *St Mark's Review*; *Studio*; *Talents*; *Verse*; *The Weekend Australian*; *The West Australian*; *Westerly*; *The Western Review*; *The Western Word*; *Writing Australia*; and *Zadok Perspectives*.

Many poems were also published in the following anthologies:

Summerland: A Western Australian Sesquicentenary Anthology of Poetry and Prose (University of Western Australia Press, 1979); *Playing With Fire: A natural selection of Religious Poetry* (Dublin: Villa Books, 1980); *Quarry: a selection of contemporary western australian poetry* (Fremantle

Arts Centre Press, 1981); *Hemisphere Annual — III* (ACT: Commonwealth Department of Education, 1982); *Instructions for Honey Ants and Other Poems* (Mattara anthology; University of Newcastle, 1983); *An Anthology of Christian Verse* (Adelaide: Rigby, 1983); *Indo-Australian Flowers* (Mangalore: Chetana Books, 1984); *Poem of Thanksgiving and other poems* (Mattara anthology; University of Newcastle, 1985); *POEMS Selected from The Australian's 20th Anniversary Competition* (Sydney: Angus & Robertson, 1985); *Inside Poetry* (South Melbourne: Pitman, 1985); *Portrait: a west coast collection* (Fremantle Arts Centre Press, 1986); *The New Oxford Book of Australian Verse* (Melbourne: Oxford University Press, 1986); *Anthology of Australian Religious Poetry* (Blackburn: Collins Dove, 1986); *An Inflection of Silence and other poems* (Mattara anthology: University of Newcastle, 1986); *Australian Poetry 1986* (Sydney: Angus & Robertson, 1986); *Zbornik Avstralskih Slovencev - 1988: Anthology of Australian Slovenes – 1988* (Sydney: Slovenian-Australian Literary & Art Circle, 1988); *Margins: A West Coast Selection of Poetry, 1829-1988* (Fremantle Arts Centre Press, 1988); *Australia Antologio* (Pizo, Italy: Edistudio, 1988); *Celebrations: A Bicentennial Anthology of Fifty Years of Western Australian Poetry and Prose* (Nedlands: University of Western Australia Press, 1988); *Wordhord: A Critical Selection of Contemporary Western Australian Poetry* (Fremantle Arts Centre Press, 1989); *Christmas Crackers: Australian Christmas Poetry* (Norwood: Omnibus Books, 1990); *Chapters into Verse: Poetry in English Inspired by the Bible – VOLUME TWO: Gospels to Revelation* (Oxford: Oxford University Press, 1993); *Whispering in God's Ear: A New Collection of Poetry for Children* (Oxford: Lion Publishing, 1994, 1996, 2004); *Summer Shorts 3* (Fremantle: Fremantle Arts Centre Press, 1995); *The Lion Christian Poetry Collection* (Oxford: Lion Publishing, 1995, 2001, 2005); *Sudden Alchemy* (Cottesloe: Fellowship of Australian Writers, 1998); *No Strings Attached* (North Paramatta: Eremos Institute, 1999); *The Yellow Star of Life* (Nollamara: Life Ministries, 2003); *The Indigo Book of Modern Australian Sonnets* (Charnwood, ACT: Ginninderra Press, 2003); *First Australian Haiku Anthology* (Australian Haiku Society/ Paper Wasp, 2003); *The Finishing Post: The Winners from the Grand National Poetry Stakes 1979–2002* (Bassendean, WA: Access Press, 2003); *The Best Australian Poems 2005* (Melbourne: Black Inc, 2005); *Studio*; (Albury: Studio, 2006); *The Best Australian Poems 2006* (Melbourne: Black Inc, 2006); *The Road South: An Anthology of Contemporary Australian Poetry* (Bengal Creations Pvt Ltd, 2007); *GROW: Under the Southern Cross* (Kenmore, Qld: Writerlynks Grow, 2008); *Unborn Beauty:*

Celebrating Pregnancy and Parenthood (Inala, Qld: Wombat Books, 2008); *Even Before You Were Born: A Christian reflection on pregnancy* (Capalaba, Qld: Even Before Publishing, 2009); *All creation sings: Psalms of Everyday Christians, Volume 1* (Capalaba, Qld: Even Before Publishing, 2010); *22* (Perth: writingWA & the Department of Education, 2010); *Australian Poetry Since 1788* (Sydney: University of New South Wales Press, 2011); *The Quadrant Book of Poetry 2001–2010* (Sydney: Quadrant Books, 2012); *The Turnrow Anthology of Contemporary Australian Poetry* (University of Louisiana at Monroe, USA: turnrow books/ ULM Press, 2012); *Notes for the Translators: from 142 New Zealand and Australian Poets* (Macao: Association of Stories in Macao, 2012); *None So Raw As This Our Land: Seventeen West Australian Poets* (Macao: Association of Stories in Macao, 2012); *Notes for the Translators: from 142 New Zealand and Australian poets* (Macao: Association of Stories in Macao, 2012); *Australian Love Poems* (Carlton South: Inkerman & Blunt Publishers, 2013, 2014); *When the Moon Is Swimming Naked: Australasian Poetry for the Chinese Youngster* (ASM Poetry/ Association of Stories in Macao, 2014); *Prayers of a Secular World* (Carlton South: Inkerman & Blunt Publishers, 2015); *Prayers of a Secular World* (Newick : Read How You Want, 2015); *Falling and Flying: Poems on Ageing* (Blackheath, NSW: Brandl & Schlesinger, 2015); *The Fremantle Press Anthology of Western Australian Poetry* (Fremantle: Fremantle Press, 2016); *The Turning Aside: The Kingdom Poets Book of Contemporary Christian Poetry* (Eugene, Oregon, USA: Cascade Books, 2016); *Contemporary Australian Poetry* (Puncher & Wattmann, 2016); and *Australian Poetry Anthology: Volume 7, 2019* (Melbourne: Australian Poetry Ltd, 2019).

Some poems were also broadcast on *A First Hearing* (Australian Broadcasting Corporation), *The Poet's Tongue* (Australian Broadcasting Corporation); *Poetica* (Australian Broadcasting Corporation); *Writer's Radio* (Radio 5UV, University of Adelaide) and Twin Cities 89.7 FM (Edith Cowan University).

The Poiema Poetry Series

COLLECTIONS IN THIS SERIES INCLUDE:

Six Sundays toward a Seventh by Sydney Lea
Epitaphs for the Journey by Paul Mariani
Within This Tree of Bones by Robert Siegel
Particular Scandals by Julie L. Moore
Gold by Barbara Crooker
A Word In My Mouth by Robert Cording
Say This Prayer into the Past by Paul Willis
Scape by Luci Shaw
Conspiracy of Light by D.S. Martin
Second Sky by Tania Runyan
Remembering Jesus by John Leax
What Cannot Be Fixed by Jill Pelaez Baumgaertner
Still Working It Out by Brad Davis
The Hatching of the Heart by Margo Swiss
Collage of Seoul by Jae Newman
Twisted Shapes of Light by William Jolliff
These Intricacies by David Harrity
Where the Sky Opens by Laurie Klein
True, False, None of the Above by Marjorie Maddox
The Turning Aside anthology edited by D.S. Martin
Falter by Marjorie Stelmach
Phases by Mischa Willett
Second Bloom by Anya Krugovoy Silver
Adam, Eve, & the Riders of the Apocalypse anthology edited by D.S. Martin
Your Twenty-First Century Prayer Life by Nathaniel Lee Hansen
Habitation of Wonder by Abigail Carroll
Ampersand by D.S. Martin
Full Worm Moon by Julie L. Moore
Ash & Embers by James A. Zoller
The Book of Kells by Barbara Crooker
Reaching Forever by Philip C. Kolin
The Book of Bearings by Diane Glancy
In a Strange Land anthology edited by D.S. Martin
What I Have I Offer With Two Hands by Jacob Stratman
Slender Warble by Susan Cowger
Madonna, Complex by Jen Stewart Fueston
No Reason by Jack Stewart

www.ingramcontent.com/pod-product-compliance
Lightning Source LLC
Chambersburg PA
CBHW031426150426
43191CB00006B/407